X

X

the mays | XX

GUEST EDITED BY
John Darnielle
Sebastiano Barassi
Tao Lin
Toby Litt

V
VARSITY PUBLICATIONS

Varsity Publications Ltd
Old Examination Hall
Free School Lane
Cambridge CB2 3RF

First published 2012 by Varsity Publications Ltd

ISBN 978-0-902240-42-1

Designed and typeset
in Calluna and Titillium Text
by Donald Futers

Printed and bound
by Y Lolfa Cyf. in Talybont, Wales

Cover photograph by Lawrence Dunn

Original concept by
Peter Ho Davies, Adrian Woolfson, Ron Dimant

British Library Cataloguing in Publication Data
A CIP catalogue record of this book
is available from the British Library.

Further copies of this book and other titles in the series can be bought through most booksellers or direct from Varsity Publications at the address above or at:
www.varsity.co.uk/mays

Contents

CINEMAYS

VISUAL ART

PROSE

Editorial Team

EDITOR
Andrew Griffin

DEPUTY EDITORS
Jessica Ballance and Kath Powlesland

DESIGNERS
Donald Futers and Joe Robertson

MANAGING EDITOR
Michael Derringer

POETRY COMMITTEE
Jack Belloli, Jo Davis, Brendan Gillott, David Grundy, Charlotte Keith, Samantha Marrah, Camilla Walker

PROSE COMMITTEE
Jenny Bottomley, Fleur Clarke, Jane Evans, Lise McNally, Peter Richardson, Matt Russell

VISUAL ART COMMITTEE
Molly Gavriel, Kirsty Gray, Holly Gupta, Praveen Paranagamage

CINEMAYS COMMITTEE
Maria Dimitrova,
Fleur Clarke, Matt Russell

WITH SPECIAL THANKS TO
Jenny Bottomley, Tristan Deveney,
Maria Dimitrova, Kirsty Gray, Camilla Walker,
Chenting Zou

×

WE ARE GRATEFUL
TO OUR COLLEGE SPONSORS:

CAMBRIDGE
Clare Hall, Fitzwilliam College, Gonville & Caius College,
Jesus College, King's College, Magdalene College,
Newnham College, Queens' College, Trinity College

OXFORD
All Souls College, Christ Church, New College,
Oriel College, Somerville College,
St Hugh's College

General Introduction

Andrew Griffin

The *Mays* is now 20 years old, and boasts a large and successful set of alumni. It is in terrible danger of becoming an institution. But as the writing in this anthology shows, even the dustiest and coldest of institutions are filled with the creation of new and innovative art: the writing collected here by students at Cambridge and Oxford universities represents some of the most innovative, urgent, vibrant and brilliant work being created today.

It is so common to express surprise in the early pages of this book that it'd be shocking if I didn't. But the fact that people are still writing, and that you're about to be reading, such spirited and witty work should be enough to humble even the most rapturous of prognosticators of the literary End Times. People keep living, and they keep writing.

In the following pages is some of the most exciting work and art being made today, by people who I've no doubt will help decide what the future of art looks like. That future, from the pieces collected here, looks disturbing, animated, vibrant and caring; most of all, it looks strange.

poetry

EDITED AND INTRODUCED
by John Darnielle

Introduction for Poetry

John Darnielle

Nagging romantic questions seem to sit on the shoulder of anyone who reads poetry. Did people use to care more about this stuff than they now do? Does it matter if anyone cares, so long as I do: so long as we do? Should the poem speak to the elusive common reader, who has never existed but who seems a fine fellow all the same, or is it all right if the poem addresses itself exclusively to those who've already seen it naked? The world has busied itself creating new distractions since the days when William Blake piped a song about a lamb and a child nearby or within wept to hear: what now from poetry in this noisy world?

The common tack when introducing a volume of poetry is either to contend that the art is healthier than is generally assumed, or that it's just as sick as you've heard but here are some salves for the wound if the world will only have them. But poetry is eternal; we have been doing it since we lived in caves; it can be no more sick or well than speech. What people mean when they decry the state of poetry is that what poetry they've seen of late has failed to reach them, to speak to them, and that they think a poem hasn't done its job if it hasn't extended a hand across that gulf between the page and the eye.

To some extent they are right. Famously, where I'm from anyway, Archibald MacLeish has contended that 'a poem should not mean | but be,' but this is easier to say than to accept when confronted with a page that seems bent on keeping secrets. We read in the hope that something will be revealed to us; and, raised from birth on the visual image, we ask that we not have to work too hard at grasping that revelation. Poetry tends, now, to stymie these hopes, or to tease us for having them. We fear and resent an imagined interlocutor calling us rubes if we haven't understood what we read.

And yet in the stillness of the poem, in that moment apart from the world, outside of time and inside a conversation which has been going on since our kind first formed words, we find a place where, if we choose, we can defer our expectations and hear the voice of another articulating its singular song. If we don't understand, we can wait; we can try harder; we can choose to remain in a state of unclarity for a moment or two, and see if there's anything there for us. A poem's atomic weight is infinite; we can mine it forever. It shouldn't have the capacity to reach us, not any more, not through all the static. Its stillness should remain still, dead amidst so much action. *Eppur si muove.*

I do tend to favor poems which are willing to meet me halfway in the gap between storytelling and the incomprehensible cry of the spirit. The poems you're about to read are in verse or they're not, but each seemed to me to find a rhythm it was willing to share, and to locate somewhere along the line that eventual clarity common to good poems old or new. In this clarity, for me, is a moment of communication: neither telling nor being told, but the opening of a line in which both take place at once, individually and dually, in a held moment. Song-hearing children who've grown up may recognize this place as the one thought lost, the one A.A. Milne located halfway down the stairs. That place abides in the poem. Long live those who find and keep that place.

John Darnielle sings with The Mountain Goats. Their most recent album is All Eternals Deck. *He blogs at* lastplanetojakarta.com, *and published* Black Sabbath: Master of Reality *in 2008.*

Phoebe Dickerson

Other Side

Last night, walking home (and the deep
blue sky hanging, stretched tight
between branches and rooftops)
My gloved hand held in his bare one,
I turned to the old folks home on
the other side of the road (with the pots
of geraniums and fairy lights in windows)
And thought of her, alone in her room,
Looking out.

And that instant – and for a while after –
All I could feel was the hand that held mine,
Firm and constant. And my ribs
Unfastened themselves, and opened,
a window to an aching sky.

Phoebe Dickerson

Here

About this pale-faced region of the moon
Dust shadows blaze the arcing midnight sky.
In sharp three-cornered crystal-coloured haze
They catch the fleeting arrows of the light
And shoot out visions that betray the night
In all its seeming star-cut black array.
In particles of severed second sight
The eyes of demons, birds and angels glint
And throw and spin their spirit souls among
The wings of beetles, and the startling songs
Of many-throated airborne mysteries;
Shell beauty, cosmic dust of wish and bone
Whisper their high-pitched symphonies;
Tunes of notelessness and wingless dreams,
Unfastened from the minds that gave them flight
And left to float among the frantic skies at night.

Ada Gafter-O'Higgins

Cock
y smile,
as if I were
a waitress
in a cream brothel.
Or a mother who
would do anything,
even this,
for her son.

Robyn Lowe

Fragment

Paint me a window of fresh freesia buds of nylon
    curtains patterned
with dinner plate paper moons and blueberry
    fields of meadow flowers
new in spring sunshine from yesterday's patio sun
    trap afternoon tea
and cake Chopin recital with fewer of our friends
    than last time when
we danced all night to that song that none of us
    knew but did by the
morning in the square when the musicians went
    quiet because of
raised voices which came like thunder pouring
    through the window
you left open and the suitcase soaked through so
    all of our clothes
were gone and we were alone together like last
    year naked before the
tree in the garden blew down and the seasons
    turned.

Richard O'Brien

Actaeon

It's tearing me apart – and not just now –
before, I mean, the skin and teeth.
It's had its fangs in me for weeks;
I wake up with my tongue bright wet with blood
and something savage in my skin.

Would you have done it if it had been him?
The man's more stag than me; that A-Team chest
is hairier than mine will ever be.
You'd keep him whole, you'd drop that sheet
and have them leave you locking horns –

but me, I pushed the curtain back and fawned
on you, your whiteness water-pearled;
I had no eyes for all your serving-girls
and soon I had no eyes, no guts, no heart,
I glutted them with longing burst when bitten.

That time you took my tongue from me, unbidden.
If I had it back I'd do it all again. Some days
I chew my arm off just for practice,
send you cards that say: you are invited to
The Donner Party. My place. 8pm. RSVP.

ACTAEON

What I mean is, I would happily and knowingly
allow you to devour every inch of me,
or even just a pinch of me, to claw me limb from
    limb
and pincer me or water-board me, stick me
with my quills but stick with me. I'm only flesh;

a bloody mess you wash off, then zip up your dress.
Now I am the man with the flailing hands,
I am the man with the frothing hounds,
you are the girl with your thighs untanned,
I am the boy with the cloven hooves,

skittering loose as the landscape moves
and falling into the furious pack
because I was the boy who could not look back.
Delirious antlers explode from my head.
I am the artist and my hands are red.

Jack Shackleton

The Jellyfish

It is a pulse. A pulse that rises
slow as sap. A pulse like clockwork
sealed in a case, a sleepy
glassy chamber pumped with ether.
There is no rush. There is the throb
of ageless organs too perfected
to evolve. And did the water
thicken spontaneously and clump
like particles inside a well
of electricity? Like syrup
globing through a thinner liquid?
They petrify us and they bloom
like an aroma, smothered with poison.

When the sea folds up its surface
and unmasks its rot, they are
deflated. They palpitate with air;
a broken vacuum like a bell
with all its brass and panic drained.
Once, I found one on the sand,
a cataract, a piece of glass
that time had seeped translucent, thick,
and indistinct. I looked into it

and it turned my face horrific
and unrecognisable. It stung me
and it hurt. It meant to hurt.

Jack Shackleton

The Paper Plane

mute. This thing is only shape,
is nothing but the matchless creases

on a finger; if we read them
with a needle, would there be music?

It was made to fit. It fits
the gap in the air like lungs in ribs,

and has a memory. The words,
the pressure of words that lie like salty,

dried-out lakes or fades of acne
that it felt through others. It has

a plan of every transformation,
it could unshake itself into

a tissue-tender crane, a ship
though rudderless, could tell our fortune.

Now it hangs a clear, birdlike,
marrowless bone, the top of its curve

where everything is neutral. Will
it fall and, like us, lie inside

its shadow? Or undo itself
and shoot indifferently as sunlight,

fateless

Scott Annett

Cranes

Slip so slow
Low as the flight
The necks
Simple like
Water which isn't
At all

Easy now
Nothing to see
They lean
Seeing me
Sliding fist-fighting
The fog

Every sound
Seeping across
The pause
Couldn't bear
Speaking because
Because

Cranes but so
Slow in the sky

CRANES

The wings
Cutting light
Traces of smiles
And I

Slip so slow
Low as the night
The light
Simple like
Water which isn't
At all

Susie Cronin

Teaching a Tiny Man to Swim

Your flat narrow belly is only the width
Of the palm of my hand barely
propping you,
you're a puny pinch safe from plunging –
And the waves they're only as
c h o p p y
As this trembling fingernailed diving board
And my smiling empty threats of
Letting you go.

Rowan Evans

from return songs

That this too is
distance

london hymns

her buoyant
with moth-

luck to earth

    via cordite
            rungs

That emmaus is
like this

    yarned rest
    wheel of

sparrow & hair

    & drum

but john
precious in joy

i see now

    every
    sung

Rowan Evans

i the crew of henry tudor

first from what wreck
did we summit

mother aquarelle?

    mary rose

she figuring me out
of the sunken work

into tense woke i
& shivered from that trestle

heart fields open
summer caves grow

ing from my back o
mother making time.

bound in transit terns
crystalize like some eye

drawn from the birth place

sun warms dry
her lash print it's

the twentieth sung
thing from memory

refracted colour
speaks the rolling

arc you held.
so determined is love

the very alloy of it

    o she an
    other ark

Rowan Evans

from rains

& tenser falls

puncturing
firwood as before

                in ancient
                -ness o

myth if

        station
        -d subkiss

would sing
my weight in

                pollen

rain looked
nude to
                toucheth hills

they smoke

whereas ground
worried blush at O

if where water
was could be
here

(quadrant stone who
yields you silvers)

why then

wet spoker

in the whole earth's afternoon

Georgia R. Wagstaff

schmetterling.

indeed, it was the original observations of mimicry that helped frame the concept of natural selection . . . your heart may pound, or you may have butterflies in your stomach. this is perfectly normal.

Black Hairstreak

Purple Hairstreak

Silver-studded Blue

in their short adult lives when they briefly add their brilliant flashes of airborne colour to the world.

YOU Almond-eyed Ringlet,

YOU False Grayling,

YOU Painted Lady,

YOU Peacock,

YOU Scarce Swallowtail!

the summer of no butterflies, with its

Brimstone

and I will become a

White-letter Hairstreak.

Alexander Freer

24 Missiles

Kingfisher, Wasp, Cardinal, Matador,
Jupiter, Bulldog, Petrel, Condor,
Sidewinder, Stinger, Sidearm, Skipper,
Blue Eye, Viper, Perseus, Ripper,
Sea Lance, Pershing, Mauler, Big Q,
Tomahawk, Patriot, Trident, Trident II.

Alexander Freer

'Preliminary Communication' (1893)

An attack will occur spontaneously,
just as memories do in normal people;

– a sleeper cell, sealed away
slick as polaris, portable as scud –

it is, however, possible to provoke one,
just as any memory can be aroused
in accordance with the laws of association.

A door slammed in the wind, the smell
of wet cattle, or anything small enough
to find unexpectedly in a pocket:
beech nuts or corroded nails, artifacts
of pain.

It can be provoked either by stimulation
of a zone or by a new experience which sets it going
owing to a similarity with the pathogenic experience.

Not the place where it began – bare floorboards,
lavender sheets, the map of a very different world –
but the experience of place: these extremes of being

we can only pretend to recover from; that draw
the shape and weight of who we are.
Like water finds familiar paths, like buildings crack
down stress lines, the patient logic of dreams
lines up fractures, consolidates the wounds.

We hope to be able to show that these two kinds of
determinant,
though they appear to be so unlike, do not differ in
essentials,
but that in both a hyperaesthetic memory is touched on.

Icons and images, the feeling
of something a little more than
possible, an indelible trace:
when light strobes through train windows,
or in the rusty pollen lillies leave behind
and like a blow to the skull we are instantly
nowhere at all.

Toby Lloyd

My Dream of Meeting John Berryman

Berryman finds me reading in an armchair
In the living room of a grand old Edwardian house,
Walls covered with renaissance art,
Clock beating majestically in the corner.
I am cold and losing my place in the dark.
Berryman sees this, and lights a fire
In the middle of the room, flames waltz
From orange to blue and back again.
He sits down next to me and speaks:

'When' he says 'a poet dies,
And the stars that were once his eyes
Go out, I cut off a lock of his hair
And weave it into my beard;
That is why my beard is so heavy long.
My inheritance from the greats:
My left sideburn is Virgil
My right sideburn is Yeats.'

The fire leans towards him as he speaks.
He gets up and returns with a bottle
Cradled in both arms, Madonna and child,
He holds up a finger for silence

So that we can hear
The ice in the glasses clicking
As it is lovingly bathed in bourbon.
The fire resumes its noise and then I ask:

'How many fathers back does your grief go?'
He shakes his heavy head and I can hear
The ideas all rattling about inside,
He drains his glass, and answers:
'All of them.'
He fixes on me a professorial stare.
'For Let Me Tell You This:
When Adam was kicked out of Neverneverland,
He cried the first salt tears that man had ever cried,
That slut of a wife no consolation by his side.
And when those tears hit the stony floor
They froze, and with those frozen tears
The lenses for a pair of glasses were made.
Now, many thousands of years after,
A doctor gave a pair of spectacles to me
And said *you'll need these, pal, if you want to see.*'

Berryman turns at last his attention to my reading:
It is one of his poems, and he offers to help.
We read for a while in silence,
But we both know it's going nowhere.
Berryman takes from his pocket a small,
Mercilessly sharp knife. Gently he makes
An incision in the poem's centre and oh-so-softly
Lifts up the flaps of its chest. Underneath I can see

The cogs turning in perfect order and
The rhythms make sense at last. And then I see
Henry, finally naked, shading his eyes from
The lights of the fire, and he never looked lovelier.

Berryman sees that I have seen
The things he wanted to show me
And that professorial stare relaxes into a smile.
He puts his hand on my shoulder.
'Let me show you something else.'
He leads me down some stairs and throws open a door.
'This, my friend, is the library!'
There are no bookshelves or even books,
Just towers of loose paper, millions upon
Millions of pages; they are holding up the ceiling.
A few scraps fly about in the wind from the door.
Berryman sits down despairing, eyes to the floor,
One hand on Yeats, the other on Virgil.
'The greatest minds that ever lived
Worked together to make this rotting mess.
What good, in the end, is a room full of words?'

And this is where it always ends, Berryman's head
Without warning explodes, coating the wall behind
    him
In comforts and terrors,
His face is still cupped in his hands.
I take my first steps back up the stairs
On tentative, fatherless feet. The fire has all gone out.

Tim Waters

Enter

This one relayed convex natural reason, momentary
tension citing other impacts, but individually clear

as a raindrop another enters, miming in gasoline:
'individual rights'; 'Kleenex filtered bright skin'; 'wars
    smooth as satin';
'here I stand, I can'; with a lighter and spray can to itself

another over   cobalt lyric shakes
white flakes   private as the swallow drops
into its proper plot.

James McKnight

Fragment

– he seems to me god-ridden
who has gannet half the night,
who has eaten half its burn.
That right holds to mile hold
his body-mile next yours.

Your hearing body
that lips his words;
that eats his words
that eat my words.

And quiet of listen turns laugh:
damp reddish reed-hair in ribs
spools tight, that quites in chest,
is wing-beaten breast.
Is blind eyes blind for looking.

Tongue-broken, listen,
hear his fire-words.
Inside my mouth
is ash unburned.

FRAGMENT

Rush of sweat is water above
the sick-fire near-breaking skin
woke under. Yoke me, Pale Grass,
take pale body that, longing,
cannot endure, but must –

cineMAYS

PRESENTS

A GRAPHIC SHORT
by Lewis Wynn

Lewis Wynn

Dawn and Dusk

ALL MEAGRE, ALL HOPEFUL...
THE GREY DIN RISES.
THE GASHOLDERS STAND FIRM, WATCHING THE CITY.
OTHERWISE, DUST LINGERS.
KFC
BRICKS AND MORTAR PERPETUALLY FALLING.
PIECE BY PIECE, DAY BY DAY,
LONDON IS FALLING

IT TOOK A WEEK FOR ANYBODY TO NOTICE.
NOW NOBODY NOTICES ANYTHING EXCEPT THE DUST.
IT SHIMMERS IN THE SUN...
AND MAKES NIGHT LIGHTER.
NOW NOBODY SPEAKS...
LIPS SEAL, EYES SQUINT.
LONDON HAS NEVER SHOWN ITS FACE, BUT NOW IT IS JUST AN EDGE, A VAGUE HAZY BLOCK, AN IMBECILE PANTOMIME BEHIND THE DUST OF ITS OWN SELF-DESTRUCTION.

NOBODY KNOWS WHY IT FALLS,
NOBODY DARES QUESTION.
THE FISH MARKETS HAVE MOVED INSIDE.
CARS LAY LOCKED AWAY.
24 HOUR
PARKING
EVERY NOW AND THEN...
PILES OF DUST SWIRL UPWARDS...
A GREAT MIST LEAPING TO THE HEAVENS...
AND THE CITY IS REVEALED.
THEN EVERYBODY REMEMBERS,
REMEMBERS EVERYTHING.

IN A CITY THAT HAS NO FUTURE, EVERYBODY LIVES IN THE PAST.
MEMORIES SPILL THROUGH THE STREETS,
UNTIL EVERYWHERE IS A DREAM...

THE MIST IS A CLOUD OF FORGETTANCE.
SITTING IN BEATEN SOFAS,
PEOPLE START SPEAKING TO THEMSELVES.
RELIVING OLD CONVERSATIONS, OLD SCENES,
OLD EMOTIONS.
AS SOON AS THE SUN GOES DOWN
THE SLOW MUMBLES OF VOICES RISE.

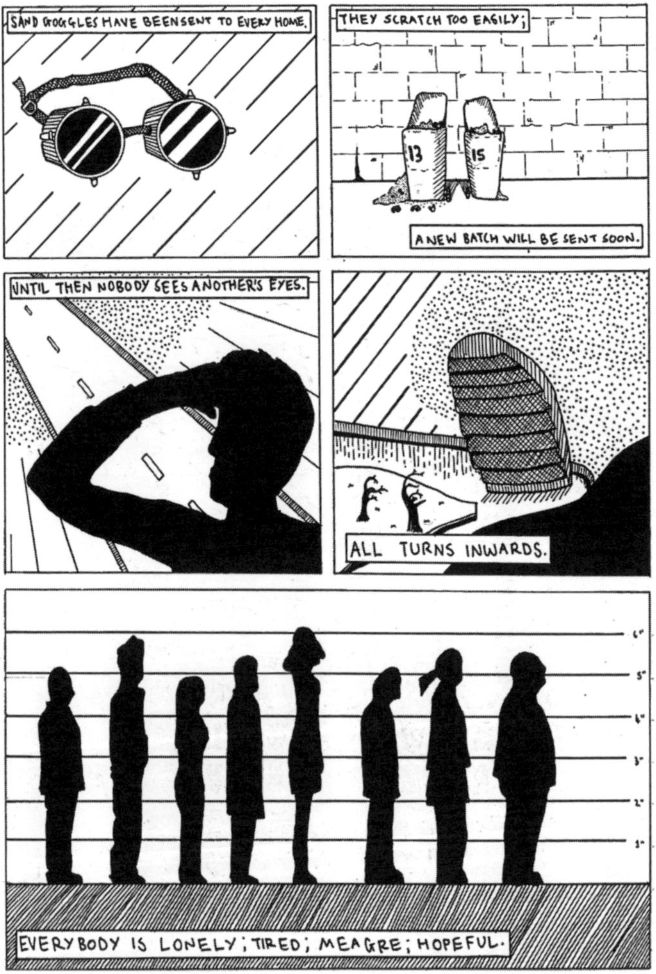
SAND GOGGLES HAVE BEEN SENT TO EVERY HOME.
THEY SCRATCH TOO EASILY;
13
15
A NEW BATCH WILL BE SENT SOON.
UNTIL THEN NOBODY SEES ANOTHER'S EYES.
ALL TURNS INWARDS.
EVERYBODY IS LONELY; TIRED; MEAGRE; HOPEFUL.

BUT NOW WE WATCH THE MORNING PLAY ITS PRELUDE.
DREAMS FLUTTER FOR A FINAL MOMENT,
LAMENTING THEIR INEVITABLE PASSING.
THEN THE DAY BEGINS,
AND LONDON RISES.

THIS IS LONDON'S STORY;
THE HOPES AND FEARS OF THOSE WHO DREAM IN DUST;
THE MAD MUTTERINGS OF THOSE WHISPERING INTO THE SLOW STREETS;
THE TALE OF THOSE LIVING IN A FALLING CITY.

visual art

EDITED AND INTRODUCED
by Sebastiano Barassi

Introduction for Visual Arts

Sebastiano Barassi

Historically the arts have tended to respond to economic and political instability by opening up and becoming more outward-looking. This is a phenomenon we are witnessing again today, in reaction to the deep social transformations and reshaping of our ways of living triggered by the financial crisis that started in 2007.

After decades of introspection and a predominant focus on the self, the arts seem again intent on engaging with significant social issues. Collaborative work practices are increasingly common, driven by the need to join forces and pool resources at a time when the latter are scarcer, but also as a way of acknowledging the importance of abandoning individualistic approaches. More broadly, we are seeing a return of well-tested artistic strategies designed to engage with, and reflect upon, challenging political and social circumstances. For example, artists increasingly look back to the past and to history in search of the best way forward; or they dispassionately record the present and its contradictions to draw attention to the scale of the problems we are facing. We are often presented with forms of social commentary, animated by varying degrees of moral and political judgment. We also see a renewed and ever more frequent tendency to engage with the 'other' – whether an audience or a social group – as a way of giving artistic practice political and social relevance. Environmental concerns have also become more central, through intellectually challenging, research-based practice or as a result of the returning interest in the recycling and reuse of materials.

Increasingly, we are also witnessing a retreat from conceptualism coupled with a return to a focus on pure form and more conventional techniques, suggesting in some cases a desire to concentrate on a traditional, almost escapist idea of art. The rejection of the perceived ugliness of the everyday also indicates an urge to create alternative, utopian realities, a sort of re-ordering of chaos reminiscent of the avant-gardes of the early 20th century. We encounter artists re-elaborating images from popular culture and challenging established modes of perception. Quite often an underlying sense of humour and fun colours even the most serious subject-matter.

These ideas inform, to a smaller or greater extent, the majority of works in this year's *Mays*. Take for example Chrystal Ding's enigmatic photographs. In their concentration on incongruous opposites they are an eloquent representation of the contradictions we face in our daily lives. The father pushing a buggy through a red-light district is a mesmerising and haunting figure. Looking a little lost and uneasy, vulnerable like his baby child, his clothing seems designed for protection from hostile surroundings – almost a modern version of the valiant medieval knight. It is an image which tells only part of a story, and invites questions. Are father and child there for a reason, or did they just take a wrong turn? And where is the baby's mother? Does she work in this seedy neighbourhood? Uncertainty and incongruities generate in the viewer contrasting feelings, ranging from intrigue to the uncanny. Similarly, the photograph of chimneys reflected in a puddle among worn-out flagstones talks of the uneasy coexistence of two worlds, the natural and the man-made, with the former constantly trying to re-establish its supremacy over the latter. The vertiginous feel resulting from the turning upside down of the architecture creates an almost Escheresque atmosphere, at once disorientating and lucidly questioning our perception of reality.

Emma Woodward's sculptural piece relies on the combination of unlike materials and visual effects. The juxtaposition of solid and transparent elements, of organic and more rigidly geometrical forms is reminiscent of the ideas of the Constructivists. There may well be, here, an affinity with their utopianism and belief in art as a tool for reshaping and improving society by modelling an alternative reality. Even the recycled appearance of some of the piece's components could be read as an ideological statement against contemporary attitudes to waste.

Affinities with Constructivism can also be found in the work of Chloe Spiby Loh. It resembles closely

Naum Gabo's study of mathematical models as formal and philosophical sources for a new approach to art, based on a lasting faith in science as the guiding light for a socially engaged practice. The exploration of light effects that characterises Chloe's work is echoed in Louise Benson's photocomposition, although it is a much more personal and emotionally-charged image. The juxtaposition of an evocative view of bedding crossed by a shaft of sunlight and an abstract, colder, prismatic decomposition of light offers a fascinating insight into the range of our emotional responses to one of the essential components of life.

Lawrence Dunn's practice is based on a multidisciplinary approach combining his interest in music, science and visual expression – well illustrated by a recent installation at the Whipple Museum of the History of Science in Cambridge, in collaboration with Ruth Hardie and Oscar Dub. The compositional rhythms of Lawrence's photographs of architectural landscapes show undoubtedly musical qualities, in particular in the fugue-like repetition of forms.

A gentle humorous vein characterises several works in this year's submission. Alice Zoo's photograph, for example, captures the immediate aftermath of a trivial accident in a supermarket aisle, which her whimsical framing turns into a situation suspended between farcical and eerie.

Drawing in series is one of Claudia Stocker's preferred methods. The skeleton of a calf born with the head inside the chest cavity due to severe curvature of the spine belongs in a group of drawings inspired by her visits to the Museum of Zoology of the University of Cambridge and the Hunterian Museum at the Royal College of Surgeons in London.

In a sense, what emerges most strongly from this year's shortlist is one of the great paradoxes around the arts. At times of economic crisis like ours it is common for artistic work to be dismissed as less valuable than, say, medicine. Yet, it is precisely at times like these that the arts show a most remarkable ability to reinvent themselves and to respond to changing social needs and circumstances. And this always reminds me of something a doctor once said in a radio interview: 'My job is to save lives; the arts' job is to make those lives worth saving. We are both equally important.'

Sebastiano Barassi is Curator at the Henry Moore Foundation, one of the UK's leading arts charities. Prior to this, he was Curator of Collections at Kettle's Yard in Cambridge.

Jonas Leonhard Tinius

TATTOOIST
VIAGRA

Chrystal Ding

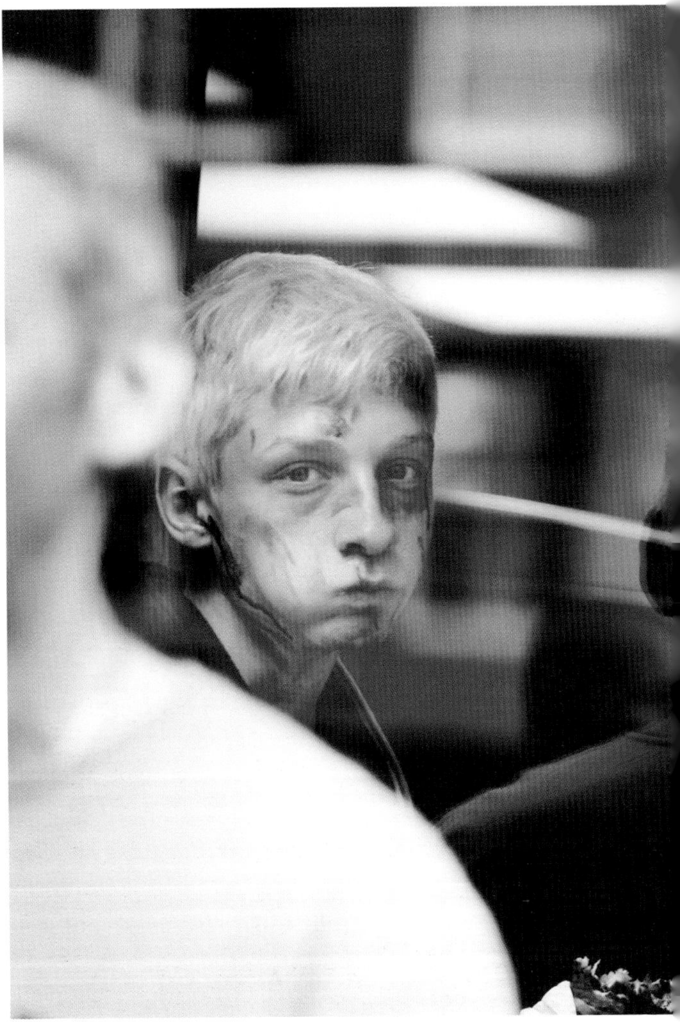

Chrystal Ding

Chrystal Ding

Emma Woodward

Louise Benson

Alice Zoo

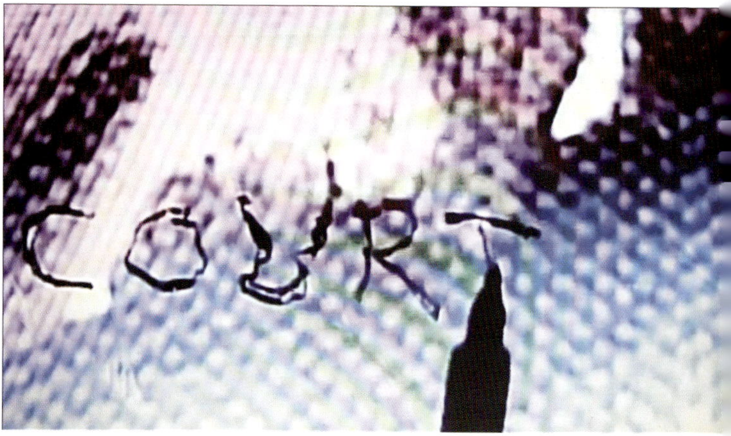

Stills from 'Courtly Love' (top) and 'Vacant' (bottom)

To see these and a selection of the other submissions to the *CineMays* category in full, visit the *Mays* website at *mays.varsity.co.uk*.

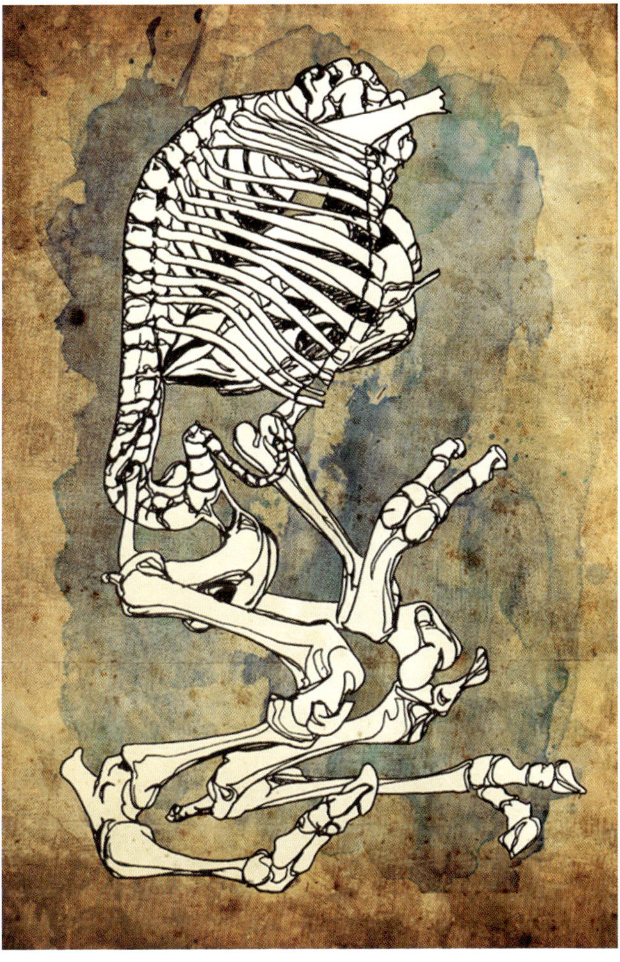

Claudia Stocker

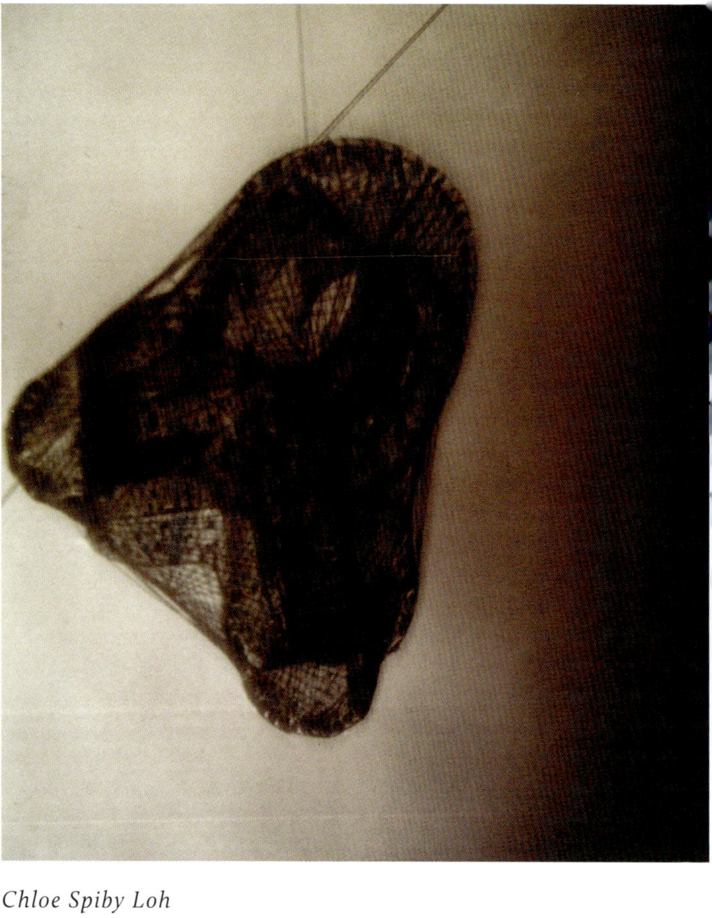

Chloe Spiby Loh

Lawrence Dunn

AND OVERLEAF >

prose

EDITED AND INTRODUCED
by Tao Lin x Toby Litt

Introductions for Prose 1

Tao Lin

This might be a British thing – I was born and live in America – but there seemed to be consistent, frequent usage of 'fucking' as a gerund in the submissions I read. Otherwise the language (and themes and tones) ranged widely. I usually wanted to read more, rather than less, of each story – the limit for submissions was 1,000 words – which seems good.

My favorites were Felix Bazalgette's funny, compelling 'The Myth of Sisyphus'; Alice Blackhurst's affectingly oblique, Amy Hempel-esque 'A Survival Story' (like an intriguing Wikipedia entry in story form); Clemmy Plemming's 'The Causeway' (about half-way through, due to its lucid and effortless-seeming prose, I sort of became aware of myself feeling like I was occupying the narrator's perspective in a Being John Malkovitch way); Encrico Cioni's amusing, thoughtful, fun/funny 'Fame'.

In 'The Myth of Sisyphus' the narrator recalls a novel that, in the world of the story, can't be found anymore:

> ... I remember now that in The Outsider the dude shot the Algerian seven times, and that that was

> considered excessive and that he had a girlfriend and his house had a little balcony which looked down onto the street, and there was this feeling of like fresh sea air all around everything . . . That doesn't make a fucking book though, does it?

The recollection ('. . . dude shot . . . considered excessive . . . feeling of like fresh sea air . . .') is evocative and interesting and, as the narrator says, 'doesn't make a fucking book.' But, I feel, it does, as its own thing, irreducible and complete, offer its own pleasures and stimulation, while also providing just enough information (not too much so as to be stifling) for a reader to imagine the book. Similarly, I was able, in a good way, to imagine the novel or movie versions of each of the aforementioned stories.

Tao Lin is an American writer, who has published two novels and a number of shorter works. He is the founder of Muumuu House, a literary press. His most recent book is Richard Yates *and he blogs at* heheheheheheheeheheheehehe.tumblr.com.

Introductions for Prose II
Toby Litt

Writers face an increasingly certain future. The inessentials of what we do, the things by which we used to be known – getting a publishing deal, having a book come out, being reviewed in the papers – all these things are evanescing. What will soon be left to writers is what we always had, words for company. Words with no livelihood attached, no career; no industry. Words with other words to left and right, above, below. Whatever else happens, within the world of publishing, within the global world, writers will go back to words – go back to words for fun, politics, consolation, self-making. Writers will dwell in and flower through and seek redemption via the arrangement, rearrangement, deletion of words. Once, this last sentence might have concluded *words on paper* or *words on the page*. These are two of the evanescent things. The words will exist on a flat, readable surface of some sort – until they migrate inside the eye itself, or back onto the breath. Mostly, for writers, the words will exist within thoughtforms: sentences, rhythms, stories, arrangements that somehow seem stronger or truer than other arrangements, very occasionally in poems. Some writers will write best by not overthinking it, others by a long Flaubertian passion or Bloomian agon or Joycean pun-upon-pun; some writers will be rewarded by the fame which makes them too busy to write, others will find a few readers and lose them, find a few more and lose them also. What is certain is that the greatest writers will be those who continue to believe most passionately in words. Not those who prettify them or are afraid to fuck around with them. But those who believe passionately arranged words (passionately fast, passionately slowly – passion is passion) are capable of anything. Capable of more, certainly, than cinema, games, drugs, sport. Words are capable of making magics – making things happen that shouldn't really be able to happen. Magics inside people's bodies. Magics in whatever part of them that would like to move towards being a soul, even if they know such a thing is impossible. Even if they know any form of magic is impossible, fake.

It's possible that some of the writers in the *Mays* have come to writing for motives that aren't entirely pure. And I'd say that's a good thing. At their age, I wasn't far from wanting what Freud said drove all artists on: 'honour, power, riches, fame, and the love of women'. Or at the very least, I wanted to have a book come out with my name on it, and for people to know I'd had a book come out with my name on it. In a sense, at this emerging stage, having mixed motives gives you a lot more to write about, makes you a lot more interesting as a writer, than just setting up shop in some vague holy magic temple of soul-creation. This doesn't necessarily mean, however, that where you and your shop end up – years later – won't be exactly that. Or something equally unexpected.

I've been asked a few times, my advice for young writers. On this occasion, I'll say this, In order to write something great, you will need the intelligence to begin and the stupidity to finish.

There's a lot of marvellously intelligent beginnings in the *Mays* – funny, atmospheric, straight, wonky – beginnings that promise, just as they should, great stupidity to come.

Toby Litt is a British author, whose eleven published novels span a wide range of genres. He is currently a lecturer in Creative Writing at Birkbeck. His most recent book is King Death, *published in 2011.*

Felix Bazalgette

The Myth of Sisyphus

The Fall, I think it was called – seemed really weird. *The Outsider*, a classic, but I have a suspicion that I didn't quite understand it as much as everyone else did. *The Plague*. That's about it. I know I read another one but I can't remember. You know – I've got a kind of notional mental picture of the books, but I read them ages ago, I can't . . . I can't remember them properly.

Have you seen a shit film starring Denzel Washington called *The Book of Eli*? Firstly it's deeply depressing that you may well have seen that film, but that you'll never read anything by Camus. I mean it's depressing that anyone had to see that film, bullshit piece of religious propaganda. I swear religious 'art' used to be good, like frescoes and stuff. What happened to that? Now it's just idiots with guitars and crap as arse films.

Anyway yeah in *The Book of Eli*, Denzel Washington is the protector of the only bible in the world, it's like a post apocalyptic wasteland where people love killing people and destroying shit and stuff. The book he's protecting is apparently the only remaining bible in the world because after the nuclear apocalypse everyone who was left destroyed all the books because they blamed the books for the nuclear apocal – you get the idea, it's bad, it's a bad film.

But still I kind of feel a lot like Denzel, except no one noticed the apocalypse when it happened, or actually it didn't happen, but no one noticed it not happening . . . Basically none of you will have heard of him so I don't know how to start really. He was famous though, and respected. His name was Albert Camus, he was French and he was writing around the middle of the 20th century, and I read two or three of his books when I was a teenager, and then didn't think much more about him for the rest of my life. Until a few years ago, when I came to realise that he had sort of disappeared from the world - like none of his books existed anymore and any record of him anywhere had been excised completely from all places you might expect to find them.

Nothing in libraries, on the internet, and in people's minds, their memories – nothing. *No results found, refine search.* It's not like people have forgotten him, it's just like he doesn't exist anymore. As though the thread had been gently, quietly unpicked, and thrown away. I don't know why it happened. I don't know why it happened.

And I don't know what to do now. I mean it's fine, we've still got Shakespeare and shit, so that's all there, we've still got everything else. It's just the fact that I'm the only one with a shred of him still in my mind . . . It doesn't make sense. Either take him away completely, without a trace, or . . . Don't leave these awkward little grains of him in my head for no reason. Do it cleanly if you're going to do it at all. What's the point otherwise?

I mean, fuck. Who am I carrying these memories for anyway? Fucking Denzel's got a final location – some organisation based on Alcatraz where this two-dimensional professor figure is building a library of all the remaining books in the post apocalyptic world . . . such a shit film . . . But you see at least he has a cargo, detailed and complete, and he's striding towards his final goal, and when he gets there they can help him unlock it, record it and reproduce it for everyone to read, he can pass it on, he's done something, he's contributed, in a tangible way, to eternity. Well, ok not eternity . . . but continuity, at least. Me . . . well . . . I'm like Denzel Washington's fuck up little brother or something. The most I could pass on to the next generation is a fucking STI.

So I keep sitting down and trying to write out The Fall, because for some reason I reckon it's the one I've got the most vivid impression of, but . . . well you can guess can't you . . . it's just shit. I feel so disgusted that I have to delete it after about two hundred words every time. Not just move to trash, but move to trash and then *empty* trash. *Are you sure you want to permanently erase the items in the trash? You can't undo this action.* And that's most of my time now. Write, delete, write, delete. Even as I start I know it's futile, but I still start, I don't know why, I can't stop starting, just in case.

Because some days it feels a little less impossible. Like I remember now that in *The Outsider* the dude shot the Algerian seven times, and that that was considered excessive and that he had a girlfriend and his house had a little balcony which looked down onto the street, and there was this feeling of like fresh sea air all around everything . . . That doesn't make a fucking book though, does it? And I know it's ok because we've still got Shakespeare and shit – but still I can't stop thinking about it.

Felix Bazalgette

Bleach

'I apologise for having to revert to this lewd orifice, 'tis my muse would have it so.'

– *Samuel Beckett,* Molloy

When I like a girl this much . . . when I love her like I did, I suppose, I can find myself fixating on one aspect of her . . . And I just . . . Once I find it I just can't get it out of my head. And I'd forgotten that it was the same with her. Until now. I'd forgotten about it but then I remembered it and I nearly cried – . . . I remembered it. We were having sex once – 'fucking' – making . . . having sex, and I just, I don't know why I don't know why I just . . . She had such a nice body. Such a nice bum. I decided to . . . decided to put my finger up her arse. She . . . well, I think she liked it. But that's not the point anyway. You see, afterwards, I was in the bathroom alone, just after, and I slowly lifted my finger up to my nose, so I could – I don't know why I did it – I could see myself in the mirror looking like a fucking freak – but I was alone and I just wanted to smell it, alright? And the thing was – this was the thing – it didn't fucking smell of anything. In fact, if anything, it smelt better than my fingers normally smell, on an average day. And this is what I can't stop thinking about – How did she get that clean? How was she that clean? I mean, even her arsehole, her anus, didn't smell of shit. And that's where the shit comes out of. How the fuck did she do that? How the fu – . . . Well I was on the bus, and I just remembered that, just for a second, and then I couldn't stop thinking about it . . . and I felt like crying or something. I had to get off the bus and sit down on a bench for a while and just think. Do you know what I mean? Do you understand? You don't understand. You don't. It doesn't matter. It was just – I don't expect you to. You see I don't care about her, and I didn't even then, by the end. I don't care about her 'in that way', I don't want to be with her . . . It's just . . . What kind of person maintains that level of cleanliness? And how? It drives me mad . . . because . . . because thinking about it – thinking about her – gives me this fucking shit feeling, like a low-grade version of nostalgia that I can't get rid of once it's in me, once it's inside my head. It makes everything in my life right now feel slightly wrong, or . . . slightly off or something. Even though I know things were wrong then. It makes me uneasy, anxious . . . here. We're not on speaking terms anymore, and I've never mentioned it anyway, so I doubt I'll ever know how, how she got it that clean. It will leave me at some point, I'm sure, but till then I'll be thinking about it all the time. It's a true mystery.

Alice Blackhurst

A Survival Story

It's winter, morning, and you're walking for the first time. No crawling – just up one day, and off you go. 'He's going to be a bright one,' Mom says.

I drive you to the aquarium. Every Thursday, when it stays open until ten. You like the tidepools where they let us touch the tadpoles, the starfish and the eels.

One time you licked a fish and got us kicked out. 'The sign said they were saltwater, I wanted to be sure!' It was better than the 'Sears years,' I could only think. When every Saturday morning we would have to pay a visit to the steam irons – electricals, aisle sixteen.

×

Adam's been talking about the eels again, says the young assistant. That's the latest thing. I'm waiting for you to come out of class.

You come out wearing blue jacquard pants, not suited to the weather. Mom always makes you dress nice. 'He might need a post-it note to put his pants on, but those pants had better be fancy.' She tells you how you're handsome, how others might not twig.

In the car park we cross paths with Mr Bullivant, the

blind teacher. 'Be good, Adam, and see you after break.' 'How're you going to do that sir?' you say. 'You can't see.'

×

This week you're learning about bridges and constructions. You know, edifying things. Mom thinks it's good. Anything but eels.

A letter is sent home for us to sign; a trip planned to San Francisco, to see the Golden Gate. It's four hours away, five including the bathroom stops. Might some parents be around to chaperone?

Mom tells you to have a nice time. You're looking in your lunchbox, trying to guess its contents.

You insist – please sis – I pack the encylopedia on sea creatures. It's heavy and your backpack's fit to burst. You won't need a book to look at them, I say. They'll be right down in the water, you'll see the eels, for real. Say hi to them from me, I say, and put you on the bus.

×

You probably didn't know what to do with yourself at that height. The young assistant probably said, Adam, Adam, come back from there right now, *Adam*. It was probably getting late. I like to think the trip was pressed for time and someone said, 'come on kids, jump to it!' – and that was why you did.

×

On one holiday in Mexico, we took a day trip on a little boat where you could dive off the sides and see the coral. I watched everybody else go from the deck. I'd rather have died than be seen in a bikini. At one point I thought 'Fuck it', took my T-shirt off, and jumped. I'm in the water, no one is going to see me, I might as well let go.

The doctors said that if you'd landed one centimeter to the left or right, you would have severed your spinal cord and drowned.

×

Everyone loves a survival story, don't they? *98% of people who make the leap don't live.* I cut another clipping just the other week: 'Student Jumps from Golden Gate Bridge (*Over 1500 deaths*) and Proves He Is A Badass. We're waiting on full reports, but we do know that he's alive. Who is this guy? Well, he sure as hell's a badass, now only more of one. Most people who jump from the Golden Gate die straight off (*approximately 52 a year, one for every week*) but this guy made it seem like he just took a quick dip to cool down. Without his own account it's probably too soon to tell, but one thing is clear: damn, he's a baller.'

A campaign is in progress to add a barrier to the bridge.

×

Richard,* (*not his actual name) Brooklyn, New York

City – was kept alive by seals circling around him. He felt them brush against his broken legs. Now he says that if that wasn't a sign from God, he doesn't know what is.

Tara Pearce, Humberside, Great Britain – was having custody battles with her ex-husband. In the hospital they scrubbed faded writing off her stomach that read: 'Cause of Death, Julio.'

Angela Schumann, near Kingston, England – was wearing a skirt that day. With the wind it blew up like a parachute and slowed her pace right down.

Mario Valesquez, Tampa Bay, Florida – has said 'You just accelerate and accelerate so fast and then it stops, but when you stop you don't feel like you hit water, you feel like you hit concrete.'

Sarah Dittman, Seattle, Washington - was admitted into hospital for little more than water in her lungs.

Graham Hinchliffe, East Sussex, England, was caught thirty feet into his fall by some extending rocks. Deep within a crevasse, his cries were finally heard by a man walking his dog on the beach below. Hinchcliffe has said to keep himself hydrated, for 72 hours he sucked on rocks.

×

I asked you why you did it once. I asked you why you did it and you shrugged straight off the bat and said: 'to see the eels.' You were grinning in your wheelchair and I hated you, wanted to hurt and hit an answer out of you.

Instead I said 'ok' and brought you sandwiches - not salted - crusts cut just right.

A cartoon was on but I switched over to the news. They were talking about the looting in New Orleans. Could we really blame them? 'I mean, it's a tough one,' said an expert. 'At the end of the day, this is a matter of life and death.'

'Shouldn't it be *or*?', you asked, never one to miss a beat. And what if I were to tell you, that sometimes there was both? I kept watching the TV. *The low railings are a feature of the beauty of the bridge.*

Clemmy Pleming

The Causeway

When Gin and I were kids we used to go crabbing out on the causeway. It was an innocent kind of blood-sport. You had a fishing line wound up on a neon plastic handle, like the string of a kite, and strips of soft, fleshy bacon to use as bait, and a bucket bearing cartoon pictures of crabs that bore little resemblance to the green, armoured, ancient things we dredged up.

You filled the bucket with water from the thin stream which was the deepest part of the estuary at high tide, water which might be milky brown or murky green depending on the weather, but which always ran into the bucket clear, as the silt settled. Then you dangled your baited line over the edge, and waited.

When a crab came, and it didn't always, there was a moment of fear between bringing it up out of its native element and putting it into the secure containment of the bucket. They moved their pincers with a slow deliberateness that we took to be an intimation of crustacean revenge. Though the biggest crab we ever caught was hardly bigger than my open hand, I still had vivid fantasies of the thing crawling up my arm and latching on to my sunburnt shoulders. I could almost feel the cold, watery weight of it.

We would catch crabs until Gin got bored, and then we would let them go. I suppose there was no harm in it.

One day, the estuary was dotted with groups of other children in shorts and sunhats, though the tide was out almost too far for crabbing. A wasteland of thick mud stretched out on all sides, pocked here and there by the breathing-pores of little creatures that lived there, and marked by a darker cross where the stream ran under the causeway. There was something delicious about the mud. It was deep and inviting and pale brown like chocolate butter icing, and it would undoubtedly be satisfying to track footprints through it.

At length, a little boy wandered over to us. He wobbled on the concrete, his round dumpling of a head questing blindly from side to side as though he was scenting the air. He had a crab held in two hands, a feeble, sallow-bellied specimen with long thin legs.

'Look what I've got,' he said to Gin.

'You have to put it in water,' said Gin, who liked to think she knew about animals, 'Or it'll die if you don't keep it underwater.'

'It's a crab,' said the boy helpfully.

'Here, Jack!' said an older girl from her encampment further up the causeway. 'Stop bothering. Come and mind the dog.'

As I watched, Jack held up his unimpressive crab and twisted one of its legs out of the socket, his small eyes squinting against the sun. The segmented limb came away quite easily, and he pulled another away, perhaps for the sake of symmetry, before lobbing the mauled trophy over the edge and onto the mud. All this was conducted without the smallest sense of malice or spectacle. He would have done the same thing whether I had been watching or not. Once the crab had disappeared from view, he let the legs fall after it, and loped back to his sister.

I followed him and called out to the girl. She was still hunkered on the edge, her face turned away from me. I twisted the toes of my sparkly jelly-shoes in the dirt, trying to make it look as though I didn't care one way or another whether she answered me.

After a long pause, during which I could hear the running stream behind me, she rose, and gave me an appraising look, through eyelashes speckled with grit.

'You're not from round here.' I recognised her from the village, and remembered her name was Leah.

'Your brother's been breaking legs off crabs,' I said.

'It's just crabs,' said Leah. She picked one out of her bucket and slung it into the stream, and watched the stream of bubbles before turning back to me with a curled lip. 'Why don't you fuck off and call the RSPCA if you care so much?'

Before Gin or I could say anything, she wandered over to inspect our pile of things.

'If you care so much you shouldn't keep them in a bucket,' she said. Before we could do anything, she swung her foot and nudged our bucket over the edge, crabs and all. Leah smirked, first at me and then at Gin, and stalked away.

I would have stood, dull with outrage, until she was far out of reach, but as she passed she stepped on my sister's toes. I don't know whether it was an accident or not, but Gin gave a yelp, and without thinking I crouched on the edge of the causeway, reached down with one hand to scoop up a fistful of mud, and flung it hard at Leah's sun-tanned back. It hit her shoulder with a satisfying slap. She wheeled round, her face hard and white. At once my fury ebbed away. I had made a stupid mistake and now she was going to get me. She ran up and shoved me hard by the shoulder and I stumbled back, falling over the edge of the causeway onto the soft bank. She followed me with a shriek.

The fight that followed was short but savage, leaving the ground scarred and churned with the deep marks of flailing limbs. Leah and I stood facing each other, panting, our bodies pasted with slurry. There was a sour taste in my mouth. Then Gin grabbed my arm with a small, hot hand, and we slunk away. The crabs were long gone, the bucket forgotten and lost in the rising tide. We didn't go back to the causeway until the next summer.

Enrico Cioni

Fame

Every year, on the first of March, Godzilla comes out for a stroll and a sandwich. It is such a popular and beloved event that many of us have come to regard it as the beginning of Spring, though everyone knows of course that that's on the 21st. Or is it the 20th? I always get them mixed up.

We all get up early in the morning to deck the town with banners and festoons, and to sweep the litter off the streets, and we all put our finest clothes on, so that the village looks its very festive best when our scaly celebrity-in-residence comes out. This usually happens at eleven o'clock on the dot. Godzilla walks out of his humble home with his arm linked around that of his pretty lady-friend, Miss Midori, and the stroll commences.

Godzilla has been living among us for about ten years. He's chosen our village to retire because no one knows about it, and you can't find it on a map. Even we sometimes forget which country we're in. This is perfect for Godzilla as he made many enemies back in the days when he used to work in the movie industry. Mothra, King Ghidora, Rodan, Mechagodzilla, King Kong, and

Raymond Burr. They created all these monsters for the purpose of making them fight in front of a camera, and once the monsters were released from their contracts they didn't know what to do with their lives, so they kept doing the only thing they knew how to do, which was fighting one another. But not Godzilla. He wasn't specifically created for the movie industry, he was born from radiations caused by nuclear testing. In fact, the *first* Godzilla movie was very much a documentary, with some fancy special effects and handsome actors thrown in to make it more marketable, on account of the fact that documentaries don't sell.

Godzilla has shrunk considerably since the days of his reckless, radiating youth. But we get to see a bit of that recklessness come back to him whenever he goes out for his stroll, as the kids spend months planning and building small models of the world megacities (Tokyo, New York, Bangkok), and then line the sidewalk with them, along Godzilla's usual path. This way, in his stroll, he will inevitably trample them to bits. Some of the models are made of raw pasta, but Godzilla doesn't mind, on account of his tough and leathery feet.

In fact, Godzilla loves the kids. During his stroll, he entertains them by aiming a jet of atomic breath towards the sidewalk below him, which makes him hover a few inches off the ground. Godzilla can't roar any more, though, on account of copyright issues. Some say that his roar was actually the sound produced by a Japanese composer by the name of Ikufube Akira as he rubbed a resin-covered leather glove along the loosened strings of a double bass, but it's all lies spread by Godzilla's enemies. Raymond Burr, in all likelihood.

At about twelve o'clock Godzilla stops at his favourite eaterie, Jimmy's. It takes him so long to get there because he walks very slowly on account of his age, his cumbersome tail, and the fact that the kids have littered the sidewalk with Fusilli Tokyos and Rigatoni New Yorks. Miss Midori also walks slowly on account of the fact that it's considered a sign of good breeding where she comes from if a lady walks slowly. Or so some of the women here say, though they have never disclosed their sources.

Godzilla can't sit down, so he orders and eats his food standing up at the counter. He needs glasses to read the menu, although the precise nature of his refractive error is unknown. Once he's ordered, we all cluster around him and ask him to tell us some stories about his days as a movie star. Godzilla is charmingly shy, and he doesn't like to boast or attract attention, but he only has to do this once a year, so he indulges us. My favourite bits are when he tells us about Japan's culture. Apparently over there they have a word for when you're full but you've still got room for dessert.

Godzilla always orders an egg and mayo sandwich, and when he's done eating it, he leaves and strolls back home. Jimmy's usually closes then so that Jimmy and his staff can watch Godzilla go back home, since they didn't get a chance to see him stroll out of it on account of the fact that they had to prepare the restaurant for him.

By the time Godzilla gets back home, there is not a soul in the village that isn't following him and gaping and gawking and pointing at him and whispering excitedly to their neighbour and asking Godzilla all kinds of questions and taking photographs or even sketching him. At one o'clock on the dot, though, the party is over, as Godzilla steps his tough, leathery feet inside his humble abode.

Godzilla has to keep indoors the rest of the year on account of the fact that many of his enemies have wings, so they could spot him from above if they ever happen to fly over our village and he's out doing his shopping or something.

Jamie Patton

The Men That Will Not Be Blamed for Nothing

(or: 'not the men who will be blamed for nothing.')

You cannot remember when you last passed this place.

Poor dear says one of them. *No matt'r 'oo she was she ne'r dservd 'at.* You cannot resist stopping on your daily walk to mingle with the little crowds, the little gluts of people staring in awe at the fresh-washed paving slabs.

D'you know'er?

I'm certain you know her quite intimately now. As you stare at the slightly stained patch of stonework you . . . well, what do you feel? I have wondered about this. Perhaps you never returned after all, or perhaps you mingled with the little crowds, the little gluts of people, staring in

One of them starts. Somebody is running down the street. . . . *in her! They's buryin' 'er!* They are passing right by, you catch the shadow of a dark hearse past the corner. The crowd are on their feet, the men remove their hats and press them to their chests as they run. You follow at a distance.

handkerchief around her neck.   Terrified of the head rolling away, you fasten a

The cemetery gates are bulging with mourners but a police line holds them.

You push your way impatiently to the front. Policeman:
Did you know her, sir?
I'm certain you   you're certain you didn't pay her, yet
Mr. Ostrog? Sir?   there there they are, two polished sovereigns
I'm certain you know her quite inside out. As you stare at the little glut of
mourners on the hill where she is to be buried

Osborn
George
Buck

Hanbury
Henriques
Mitre
Miller
Clarke
Castle
Pinchin

Swas it a hill? Or
was she interred in a patch of ground unconsecrated and unmourned? Who
was there to hold her hand as life trickled down her neck
there was life in her yet when Robert Paul felt her stirring
Back, back past Buck's Row, back to your lodgings to throw yourself waking on a
thin bed or a plush bed in Spitalfields or Mayfair and laugh or groan or weep or cry,
cry weep or cry scream, triumph. You
you
you have done it, it has been started and it will be finished

But perhaps. Perhaps you only penned 'Dear Boss' wanted a have-a-go murder penfriend. Mere kidney-wrapper. Or perhaps you pulled her quite inside out, slit open the belly like a pig and rustled about her colon and womb with a workman's knife. Or it was a bayonet. You flash back, *Waiting for my friend, he's gone with a girl.* That night you were in your mid twenties, a grenadier, no medals but some good-conduct badges, you were five-foot-nine or -ten. Your friend was a grenadier, no medals but good-conduct badges, five-foot-nine or -ten as you sank your workman's knife into her thirty-eight times and put your bayonet in her heart just the once

You   we
                    must not get carried away with theories.

Martha Tabram was killed three hours after she was seen with a soldier: ample time for her to have ventured out again into Whitechapel Road or Commercial Street, found herself another client and returned to the relative seclusion of George Yard.

but the next time

she falls against the fence and you paint two lines on her neck. Hoisting her dress up you find a sealed pocket. Two combs inside, you toss it aside. Taking the blade you

sever the skin of the abdomen

working quickly there is a great mass of

heaving the intestines and dropping them to your left

There is no evidence of   you tug the rings

from her fingers   a market for organs – but theories . . .

she was wearing a handkerchief around her neck

cut out the uterus,   *Your*   finally
she is a whore and   hands
deserves this meat treatment   barely shaking, but the gore is
and place them   rings from her fingers and   shant quit ripping them
in your pocket as a grisly   till I do get buckled
she was carrying two pennies inside, you toss them aside.
Taking the blade   polished
above the vagina, then a piece of the stomach
leave it on the ground, not important
Dear   rings from her and place them at her feet
Mr. Lusk   and away,

into the London morning.
Dawn is breaking.

Did you know her?
Better than anyone.

People do stare as you leave. *Filthy foreigner.* Aapron Kosminski, Polish you take the
Jew just outta the asylum rings from her fingers and they form
Two
Beautiful brass pillars. And you line them
up with the two polished farthings that you gave her but passed off as sovereigns.

By the time the police arrive Stephen Knight
they are passing right by and I catch the shadow of a dark figure
peeringly I try to penetrate the fog of the London streets of 1888
bulging with mourners but the line holds, it holds

she falls against the fence in Hanbury Street and you double

Yours

your face is obscured event

you push up your faded top hat and wipe your fifty-year-old brow, working up a
sweat

Did you know her?
As you work on her you can see the outlines of the others, maybe faintly the
glow of the raging there is fire in Mary Kelly's room with pieces of her
placed below her head,   there is   the skin off in strips, the heart eaten or I
think burned you can see where   there is something   you will cut with your
paintbrush-knife your leyline writer   something beyond and through

You are the spirit of a time.

Know her?
glutted with crowds, there is a great mass of heaving –   perhaps   –

Yours

truly,

Emily Marchant

for E.B.M.M.

America was named after a place that her father had read about in an old newspaper. Before everyone was gone, their street had a shop, one of the last of its kind, stacked wall-high with jigsaws, magnifying glasses, typewriters and letter openers. These were things a generation had been proud of, like poetry readings and rail services. She would think of it later as a backdrop to the most vivid of her memories: her father sitting in light angled over a high, dust-thick sill, his feet planted wide and his brown hand cradling the spine of a yellowed book. Shelves ranging like a gasp into the forgotten darkness of the ceiling above him.

Perhaps she remembered the scene because it always came at the end of a search. 'Fetch your father' usually sent her there if the search lasted more than a few minutes. He and the shopkeeper didn't seem to be friends but America couldn't remember her father smoking a cigarette without him, and his fingers were yellow from tobacco.

'Your sign's peeled,' her father had said once while America was standing under the weight of his hand on her head.

'So it is.' The shopkeeper was thin, tremulous and incapacitated by his own eccentricities. Somehow everything he said conjured its own full stop. America could see words and cigarette drags moving under the skin of his neck.

'Can't make out what it says there.'

'No, sir.'

'Just the initials, S and P.'

'Silence Please. Strange Place. Somewhere Probably.'

As America walked back home with her father, he told her, with laughter in his voice, 'I've asked him that question every week for a long while, my love. He never tells the truth. I don't think even he remembers the name of the old place.'

Emma Levinkind

War

It was 2024, the year that the London Zoo admitted that there was no such thing as 'a giraffe', and for years they had been creating the exhibit by feeding deer through a mangle and press.

They knew it was barbaric, but it worked wonders for visitor numbers.

×

I had been summoned to the Prime Minister's office. When I arrived, he was sitting at the desk, smiling to himself. Taylor, the Defence Secretary, was standing by the window. The Prime Minister sighed contentedly, clasped his hands, and spoke. 'I was doing a spot of reading earlier,' he said, gesturing vaguely in the direction of the bookcase. 'Did you know that the digital photography was invented by the military? Just think, the greatest advances over the last few years – the GPS, the mobile phone, the internet – all created in the search for weapons. I know exactly how I'm going to spark innovation; Britain is going to go to war!'

'You can't be serious!' I said.

'Oh, but I am,' the Prime Minister replied. 'It doesn't

have to be massive. Just a war-let.'

Taylor spoke up. 'If you'll excuse me, sir, against whom will you be waging this war?'

The Prime Minister smiled. 'I was hoping that you'd be able to help me with that. What about the Middle East?'

'Too controversial,' Taylor replied.

'North Korea?'

'Too nuclear.'

'What do we know about Kyrgyzstan?'

'It's hard to say.'

'Finland?'

'Someone might notice.'

'The Isle of Sodor?'

'Doesn't actually exist.'

'The Isle of Wight?'

'Belongs to us.'

There was a small pause before the Prime Minister spoke again.

'Legoland! It's perfect. It's a small, land-locked republic that hasn't gone nuclear.'

I objected. 'You can't declare war on Legoland.'

'Why not?' the Prime Minister asked.

'You can't just start a war because you think it'd be useful! War is a serious matter, claiming the lives and consciences of many. It's a matter of ethical gravity; conflict leaves scars both physical and psychological on the participants and observers. When wars are entered into, it's as a last resort.'

'Well, what reason do countries usually give for

going to war?' the Prime minister asked, impatiently.

Taylor stepped in: 'Well, historically, most conflicts arise from a perceived sleight or threat. The other party might invade Poland, for example, or have carnal relations with Helen of Troy. With Iraq it was a dossier citing evidence of weapons of mass destruction.'

The Prime Minister got up from his desk, and pretended to give a speech. 'Ladies and gentlemen, thank you for coming to this press conference. It is with great regret that I announce that Britain is now at war. Legoland has the capacity to walk through Poland in 45 minutes to sleep with Helen of Troy.' He shook his head. 'No, no, that doesn't sound right at all. How about: Legoland intends to invade Helen of Troy in order to sleep with Poland, in 45 minutes?'

I had to say something. 'Sir, you cannot start a war to achieve your own ends and justify it retrospectively.'

'Would it make you feel better if it wasn't against a specific country?' he asked.

I faltered.

The Prime Minister continued, 'Yes, we could have a War on Obesity.'

Taylor chimed in, 'Would that involve a campaign of blowing up fast food joints?'

'Or how about a War on Drugs?'

'I think the soldiers would perform better if they weren't on LSD.'

'A War on Apathy?'

'No-one would care.'

'A war on seeking approval?'

'I don't know, the public might not like it.'

'A war on cliché?'

'It's been done before.'

'I've got it,' he said. 'A War on Terror.'

'But that doesn't make sense.' I said. 'You can't wage war on an emotion.'

The Prime Minister turned to face me. 'You're such a joy-killer. You can't wage war on a country. You can't wage war on an abstract concept. You can't take your trousers off now, that's the French ambassador.

'Sometimes I wonder why I hired you.'

Ioanna Mavrou

The Astronaut's Wife

The day they announced the end of the space shuttle his wife threw her own version of a hero parade.

'Finally, I can now sleep at night,' she said to him and then spent the rest of the afternoon on the phone inviting her whole family over to celebrate that from now on her husband was no longer in danger of dying in a fiery crash or in space deprived of oxygen.

She made him set up the grill in the back yard while she went out to the store and returned with enough burgers and buns to feed a small army. She brought balloons and sparklers for the kids, champagne and beer for the adults, and a cake in the shape of a big red pair of lips. (This was all she could find that looked special enough, she explained, on such short notice.)

He cooked the burgers and greeted the family and friends and watched his wife in her favourite dress tell over and over again that it was as if a great obstacle had been lifted from their lives. He didn't say anything when she toasted to 'her husband, the retired astronaut,' he didn't even hint that she had gone too far when she brought out the freeze-dried ice cream. He could see she was so happy so he didn't have the heart to tell her that he was scheduled to fly out to Kazakhstan and set off for the International Space Station in a rocket that was probably left over from Yuri Gagarin's time.

Susie Cronin

Being *Vazaha Be*

'*Maffeo-o!*' – he is coaxed through the doorframe and is tiny, his little fists balled up giddily over his scrunched eyes like conkers. His older sisters are much more diligent, Anja, practical, scraping over the best chair for the *vazaha* visitor, Gloria pouting nonchalantly, but in earnest patent and with a gold band strung across her temples. Irma, *maman*, is very much a schoolteacher even at home, but then she told me one Sunday morning she had been like that always – she'd have been an Anja, I think, smiling. The house is part-classroom, with vocabulary Malagasy-French-English in their cursive towers casting a shadow of diligence over breakfast of hacked mofo dupain ('bread bread': 'gasy *mofo* ('*moof*') followed by '*du pain*', *mofo* as the French know it – baguette), and hot milk. Jesus is always, always thanked whether for papaya, Fanta orange, soggy rice or manioc. These are set apart and too young to know it, they are children with books and with Fanta. I spot the word 'limpid/limpide': the children are five, eight and ten . . .

The Da is only ever referred to as the Pastor, he was tall and commanding, but with a boy's face, and rides a motorbike with bumper stickers plastered across in English saying things like 'God is so good!' and '. . . *Jesosy* . . .', with decorative hearts for emphasis.

Mid-conversation the light snaps out – the power cuts in Arivonimamo are more or less daily now and particularly tense out on the roads when bike spokes' creaks and zebu plods are the sole points of orientation. I learnt quickly that it was not tactful to be traipsing up the street in my head torch for salty crackers. If anything, though, darkness vivifies these streets – you can feel from habit the scrawny poultry darting, the pile of avocadoes lying on a blanket on the roadside, the exclamatory dark puddle of a small baby's damp bottom. A cut interrupted the very moment I was to meet a new friend's small siblings: unexpected, their terrified faces filled the light swelled out from two squat candles and the strike of a match.

Back to the living room and we are fumbling with candles again – I carry matches on me these days, for power cuts, for frying, for cooking my shower in a tall pot each morning, ready when it's bubbling, mixing cups of hot and cold to make clean. Neither for love nor money could I convince my newfound friends their thirsty red soil felt not so far at all from my waterlogged home turf, and the same curious eyes trying to figure out who you're related to as you walk down the street each morning.

×

In the guidebook you can read in print that a cyclone

hits Tamatave every couple of years, but clapping eyes on its crumbling stone buildings snaked with vivid green creepers will suffice. These wide, empty window frames with occasional figures passing through hold high estimations of what they must've been before their elegance drifted elsewhere. The streets are mostly empty and mostly hostile. On the horizon sits the port, and nearer, outlined by the sunset, a creaking Ferris wheel no more than twice my height whines rooted in the sand, the lightest of breezes tormenting it. And there are pineapples.

The familiar scene is as follows: a young and beautiful Malagasy girl sits at a crisply lain table, mouth closed and a neutral expression, eyes elsewhere, and with her a greying European tourist, giddy, wriggling his tongue, murmuring in French. Sometimes her sister sits with them, other times her children. As they get up to leave, her reticence is explained by an ass that slowly sways, resigned to the usual order of every pair of eyes in the place being planted on it. Younger still than I am, and yet she somehow keeps from unravelling. Seemingly in her solitude she is much more vulnerable than the lines of girls stood bored on every corner in Antananarivo, in their wedges and silver lipstick, denim jackets and velvet scrunchies. Like that you could almost hold the hope they'd all bundle off safely together at the end of the day.

×

But the cyclones will keep coming. The majority of small girls with braids will still long to grow up and be air hostesses. Orchids will ex- and implode. People will shine the floor to the sound of half a coconut tap-dancing. The sun will rise and set. Teenage boys will keep wearing floral blouses and old men will still hold hands. Dances will be danced with bones wrapped in fraying cloth. The rum may well stay like furniture polish. The place will stay ringing with voices that could break your heart in one note, but a tinny mobile phone playing 'Miss' Celine Dion, or karaoke backings for Ronan Keating will continue to turn Malagasy weak at the knees.

Tall pale men in sunglasses and polo shirts will continue to grossly overestimate ariary tips and send luggage boys whooping and leaping inwards from the pier, clutching the precious notes. I promised my kids more vazaha, and sure enough they'll get them. They'll teach the same English vocabulary with the same avocado tree clawing at the absent window panes and end each day in Arivonimamo covered in chalk. Hopefully they will make friends, and walk the ditches between the paddy fields, and wake up on occasional dreary mornings back home to careful email messages reporting on humidity and family gatherings and they will feel cradled in far-flung affection. The vazaha will probably unlearn the same things I unlearnt; note the same things as I did, struggle over Soanierana-Ivongo in its potholes and in its syllables, and sidle up gleaming white shins to the sunshine.

Jim Kitchen

Pet Shop Toys

If you've given enough thought to Elaine you will know how she will act or react in a given situation and so a plot point is born. But if she buys the mice despite her phobia for no good reason the story will not hang together. An editor will say the story isn't credible. In real life actions often have no significant results. People who hurt others go unpunished, the good go unrewarded, crimes remain unsolved and murderers walk free. We leave relationships just because that's the mood we're in. But in fiction the dialogue and actions of the characters must be logical and bear appropriate consequences. Characters should act in a consistent manner – until you build into the story a reason for them not to do so.

Elaine buys the mice.

Betty Liou

Trial 104

The 11th floor had the best view. Those who knew the city well knew that the Osiren building provided the clearest view of the sky. The tower came to a tapered point like an extended finger tracing the dark purple sky. After the earthquakes and the destruction from the Anti-Alignment movements, skyscrapers were banned. They became a myth like the pyramids, a vintage design that would resurface years later with a sense of nostalgia and kitsch. And now once again, they would become a beacon of a growing metropolis. Dr Osiren, the self-declared savior of the Omega orphans, commissioned the original design and execution to be built as a memorial for those who were eliminated. It was an obelisk of twisted Bordilaium and glass. Metal had long been depleted. Bordilaium was the closest material that could be manufactured to resemble metal; it worked great for skyscrapers, but couldn't hold up under intense pressure changes. No one had seen a plane in decades. For this very reason, people had crowded themselves into the pointy beanstalk building waiting for the results of the experiments. The cold hard exterior of the building pulsated with life as the crowd lined themselves against the long paneled windows at each floor. There was a twitching in the air, electricity mixed with sweat. The smell of perspiration made Jonathan sick. It always triggered a sense of dread, perhaps a conditioning that occurred over the last couple of years. He was used to crowds. He slept in crowds, showered in crowds, dreamed in crowds, disappeared in crowds. The touch of skin on skin was comforting, but the sweat he could never get used to. Sweat always meant death, especially when the experiments began.

Jonathan slid undetected in the sea of flesh as he pushed himself to the window on the eleventh floor. He had promised his twin brother he'd watch him from the best place possible. It was the least he could do. He wanted to see his face just one last time, if he could stomach to watch. This was the third time this month the Osiren was filled with curious spectators. People left disappointed twice before. Trials 102 and 103 were the only ones deemed safe enough to test off the ledge; both were unsuccessful. Guilt shot through him as he watched the gate slide open and Byron crept out on to the rickety plank. He should've refused his brother's offer. He was caught off guard by Byron's sacrifice, uncertain as to why he would make such a trade. He ran through the scenes over and over, something he'd done time and time again, trying to retrace his thoughts in order to figure out how he could've been such a coward. He could've just refused, let his fate play out with dignity. He tried to pull the scenes back into consciousness. There were whispers throughout the camp, whispers about the experiments, rumors floating around once again on the progress of the serum. Jonathan's number had been pulled that morning. He distanced himself from the group, not wanting to generate any false hope. There were always rumors before the experiments; none of them were ever true. He let the ringing in his ears lull him into a deep sleep. Just as he was about to drift, he felt his brother's hand on his arm. Byron gently pushed him awake. A bead of sweat rolled off Byron's brow landing on Jonathan's lip. The salty taste was enough to make him vomit; he hated the smell of sweat. He heard Byron whisper, 'I'll do it . . . I'll take your place.' With eyes tightly shut, Jonathan nodded his head in agreement. Perhaps the nausea had impaired his judgment. He just needed to sleep. The next morning, his brother was gone.

The crowd, which sounded like angry hornets, hushed into a stiff silence. As the gate closed behind Byron, Jonathan could make out the ominous inscription: 'I will ascend to the heavens; I will raise my throne above the stars of God; I will sit enthroned on the mount of assembly, on the utmost heights of Mount Zaphon. I will ascend above the tops of the clouds.' These were the same words the orphans were taught to recite night after night. The same words Osiren used as empty promises. He promised they would be heroes of a generation, amongst the first to master flight without machines. But all Jonathan ever witnessed was death, 103 times to be exact. Life always seemed to be about mastery. His parents tried to master death by trying to predict it, but they were wrong, and they paid the price for it, and now their children continued to pay the price for their mistake. Flight became the new symbol of mastery. To bend the laws of science as you please, using nothing more than the human mind and body, was the deliverance people had hoped for. It was their story of redemption. But a man rises only on the backs of other men, and in this case, they fly over the bodies of dead orphans. Byron ran off the edge, it was quick; the crowd barely had a chance to react. Jonathan stayed focused on his brother. There he went. One, two, three . . . he didn't tumble downwards like the others. Four, five, a little smile broke through Byron's pale lips. It was the last thing Jonathan expected to see. Before he could process his thoughts, he heard the roar from the crowd; the hornets began to buzz. 15 seconds, the serum never worked this well before. Jonathan felt a lump in his throat. 16 seconds, a shot of electricity tunneled through his stomach zinging up his spine. 17 seconds, he felt ashamed and let the jolt die. 18 seconds, he wanted to be happy. 19 seconds, the roar from the crowd drowned out his thoughts. 20 seconds, Byron was still in the air, still smiling. 21 seconds, time to come down.

Christina Farley

Professor Farthyng and the Bicycle

Professor Farthyng fell off the bicycle when he attempted to ride side-saddle. I remember the instigence crystally, as it was my bike he had subfuscated, and was spurtling loose-Riley down the high street on (freaming as he went) when he expunged himself straight into the path of an oncoming tram. Professor Farthying was barely sprankled, emerging scatheless from beneath the rotataries, which was more than could be said for my bicyclicle, now a twistrunkled wreck.

Jess Kwong

from The Reunion

Kimberly Dean ——— *Confirm*
Josh Meredith ——— *Confirm*
Nick Allen ——— *Confirm*
Stephanie Willis ——— *Confirm*

An old cast of characters from Northwood High reassembles on the screen and smiles at him. Josh Meredith stands in front of the Grand Canyon with an arm around his wife, sunburnt, jowls in full descent. Nick Allen grins with desperation, wearing a very wide tie. Steph Sutton-cum-Willis obscures the signs of facial decay with what appears to be a full-throated, eye-scrunching laugh, except that it was clearly taken with a webcam in a nondescript computer room after several unflattering earlier tries. Kim Dean is the most ill-preserved of all. Her thin lips look like they've been shellacked with car paint. Her hair is crisp, arrayed like tumbleweed. A flaccid face meanders between these two with the texture of a dirt road. Poor Kim. Vince searches for a vestige of his high school sweetheart, but even those firework eyes have dulled.

He has no intention of attending their reunion.

Those things happen only for the benefit of former geeks like Robbie Hubbert and Cassie Ellis-Jones, geeks who have since attained professional and familial success. From the looks of it, Robbie went to Fordham, graduated to some well-paid job in the city and now has a very pretty wife and two athletic sons (the sort of kids who wouldn't take a daily jockstrap bitch-slap with the meekness that their father did.) Cassie Ellis-Jones is nearly unrecognizable, having sloughed 60-odd pounds off her frame through some combination of diet and witchcraft. She appears to be a happily married yoga instructor. There are photos of her swimming beside a giant sea turtle, chucking up deuces before she presumably dove out of a plane, and contorting her body in various ways on the tops of hills. Cassie Ellis-Jones, who once farted thunderously in PE class and was, from that day forth, Gassy Cassie – *Gassy Cassie* is an *adventurer.* To appear before this tribunal in his slack, doughy body, with nothing to show for the last twenty years – the idea is repellent in the extreme.

Vince Teddo wipes pizza grease onto his knee. For four years he had the misfortune of being right hand man to Kyle Everett, a county legend who led Northwood to Division 1 victory two years in a row. It didn't seem like misfortune while he and Kyle held court in Northwood, but Vince suspects that peaking early set them both on an unavoidable course for mediocrity. Kyle, earnest, effortless, was scouted by Youngstown State but got beaten out in the depth chart by three other quarterbacks. He quit after freshman year. Last Vince checked, Kyle teaches PE at the Helping Hands Special Needs School. Vince himself used to be a solid enough right tackle, but as with most high school athletes he got fat the minute he stopped training and hasn't slowed down since.

Cassie smirks at him from the edge of a cliff with one sinewy leg up in the air, palms pressed together, tits ballooning out of her sports bra. Guess those stayed the same size. He thinks about the time in ninth grade when he and Kyle hung out in one of the girl's showers during lunch, hoping to catch a glimpse of them changing. The curtain bore a large yellowed water stain in the shape of Africa. It smelled like cheese and feet and there was a damp, varicolored spiral of hair in the drain, a rusty pink razor, and a bar of soap with one long pube embedded in it. Girls are disgusting, Vince thought.

He lost track of how long the two of them had been crammed in there and he had almost lost interest when Kim Dean and Steph Sutton burst in, chattering about something, and dumped their bags on the ground. Since their first day at Northwood, Kim and Steph were best friends by natural selection: each sensed that their collective beauty was more potent than its parts. Kim took off her sweater and the hem of her shirt lifted, revealing a swath of pale, creamy skin and two dimples in her back just above her butt. (One momentous night a few years later, Vince rediscovered those dimples on a couch in her dad's house.) Beside Kim, Steph Sutton gathered up her long brown hair to reveal a perfect neck, curving under her ear and resolving into jaw, cheekbone, lashes. Kyle glanced at him and Vince shifted uncomfortably. It occurred to him, as he tugged his jacket over his crotch, that they hadn't thought this one through too well. If they actually saw any naked girls, both of them would be too busy trying to fight back erections to really enjoy it. Thankfully, somehow all of the girls had mastered the skill of changing without actually being naked at any intermediary point. For a few miraculous seconds each, they twisted around in a tangle of straps and suddenly re-emerged, extracted bras from their t-shirt sleeves, and stooped to tie their shoelaces. Vince felt as though he should clap.

As quickly as it had filled up the room emptied, except for Cassie Ellis-Jones. She turned toward them, away from the door, set her glasses on the bench and reached back to unclasp her bra. Amongst the ninth grade girls Cassie alone was developed enough to actually need one. Her breasts spilled free of her bra and stared Vince dead in the eye. They were plump and high-set, nipples an impeccable pink. As she fumbled with a sports bra over her head, these marvellous, disembodied breasts shuddered side to side. Vince's mouth went dry and he felt his dick harden against his will. He heard Kyle exhale.

Absently, he reaches down. Cliffside Cassie smirks at him. This is sick, he thinks. I can't jerk off to a picture of Cassie Ellis-Jones. He slackens his pace, hunting for inspiration with his left hand. Present-day Kim is no help but Steph's picture oddly gets him going again.

Vince remembers prom night, when Kim stormed off for some long-forgotten reason; he and Steph ended up in the equipment room, where she knelt down between racks of basketballs and started rooting around in his boxers. She evidently never told Kim about it because they remained friends for years. The first time Vince saw them together after that, he felt anxious; the second and every other time, a powerful twinge of glee.

Three minutes later Vince is slumped over his chair, staring at the ceiling, catching his breath. He wonders if Kyle is going to the reunion.

Maria Dimitrova

Soft Lines, I

The buildings are textures, the skyline a fluid wave of linguistic features, entangled in knots of collective histories. In this town, the verbs are disabled, fool proof of any action. Within its core, like a broken fruit, a malady lies, growing in the shape of salt water, an oyster shook relentlessly until its brilliant fluids coalesce. The impressionist brushstrokes fall off from the canvas as the base materials get transmuted into marvels of new beauty.

Ideas need to be delegated directly and clearly. People here hate the world's complexity, there's confusion if they have to take responsibility for their actions. If you push them in the right direction, they might overcome the metaphorical gap everyone's trying to jump over and maybe even tilt. Such thoughts were occupying Aleksander Smirnenski's mind as he was driving at the edge of the city, drawn into an unstable relationship between dreams and reality. He parked in one of the slots among the dusty conglomeration of mud-walls, hillocks, dried up beetles, etc. that made up Mladost, the neighbourhood named after what used to mean youth. The shreds and tatters of the soviet bric-a-brac strangled the air, manifesting their absurd aesthetic in the muted palette of concrete blocs. Aleksander stepped out of the car carefully, fixating his attention on insignificant details that crossed his path; empty tin can, dog, the broken cubicles at the end of the square. The overpowering grayness was punctuated by fluorescent ads and logos that lit up up his path like false carriers of hope.

Mladost hadn't changed much, except all surfaces seemed to have collected more dust, with brown, sticky patches where things seemed to have been spilt. The sound of its name too, it rang old to him, like a word in a saying, progressively emptied out of its meaning. Aleksander loudly snuffed out the dust particles trying to enter his memory and headed towards the tiny kitchen window that fixed the only light on the blank facade of the infinite block. He knew Yuliya was watching him from behind the dry tea-stained curtains, following his walk through the uneven parking lot to the steel gate. The clouds were lowering down, disappearing into the brown coral hue of the buildings as the last sunrays spilled on the dystopian panels squatting in their own decay. A reductive snapshot.

Earlier that evening Alexander had contemplated missing this first family dinner and staying home with a put-on cold for an excuse. Ever since his return, he had hardly left his appartment and tried to keep the necessary ocassions to a minimum. He had tried to watch tv but didn't change the channel when something stupid came on and in bed he had tried to masturbate but felt cold and couldn't think of anything.

He cleared his throat as he walked along the paved pathway, his fingers squeezing the cellophane bag wrapped around the last-minute present. Maybe if he distracted himself long enough throughout, time will slide by quickly and it wouldn't make any difference.

He pressed the bell, ceasing Yuliya's motherly espionage as she disappeared from behind the window frame. The humid stairway welcomed him with the familiar smell of stale coffee and urine that had seeped into his memory. He pressed the cracked elevator button but decidedly took up the stairs when the light approached faster than he anticipated. The walls, decorated with torn stickers, ink scratches, and other multi-media reflections, slid past him like a reel of the life that had gone by between the floors. He was used to the mutual agreement about that ambiguous area surrounding the space between each 80 square meter apartment: a hybrid between a public noticeboard and a garden latrine, the stairs seemed like the only place that provided an arena for the two inherently human needs for release.

As he reached the seventh floor, he heard keys slide into the thin apparment door and suddenly found himself in Yuliya's effusive embraces. A plump little woman with her hair done up in a bun, Yulia was smiling at him, her face now marked by lines like cracks on a French loaf. As she stamped wet kisses on his cheeks, she loudly announced his arrival to the rest of the family who gathered in the tiny entree. Yulia quickly lifted his coat from behind his arms and carefully hung it on top of the pile as her daughters, Slaveya and Sofia, waited in turn to embrace him. He wished Slaveya happy birthday and felt the child inside her kick him as he hugged her. He kept on holding her present, not knowing what to say and do with it. He gave it to her, murmuring a greeting to everyone else sat in the living room as Sofia briskly pulled him into the kitchen.

The air was compressed with the thick vapours of tobacco smoke and cooking. He pulled a chair from under the table, taking up more of the already confined space of the room. Nothing inside had changed; like flowers in formaldehyde, surfaces were marked by no difference except to a trained eye. He looked around, re-counting the minute details from his memory: the heavy stove, the stained fridge, the table hidden under a rustic tablecloth, even the string of dried orange peelings, which their great grandmother carefully plucked into her cakes. It was precisely in this kitchen where

Aleks, Sofia and the other children were put down to dinner on every birthday, Christmas, and festive occasion, and where Grandma Tu would monitor their plates and force-feed any bites left on the edges.

The silence that now pressed between them made the hour of privacy before joining the festivities in the other room stretch to unexpected proportions. Aleksander wanted to busy himself; he saw a pile of potatoes and grabbed the rusty peeler from the table. The whole city was coming back to him, as he filled the photographic containers with his own experience with the kiosks and bleak suburbs, myopic theatre boxes and nightclubs crowded by disillusioned youth, mosque lamps, oil lamps that struck corners in a subdued glow, the cars on the sidewalks, defied by the unsophisticated definitional asphalt. Sometimes they would begin a new life, through bizare intratextual attractions and repulsions, one after the other they merge and move like shots in a film, entering into a common kinetic motion, which entices characters and events into a new story.

Sofia's attempts to begin a conversation were voluntarily interrupted, either by the necessity to mix the salad, or take something out of the fridge. Finally, she poured two glasses of voka, put a lid on one of the steaming pans, and faced him from the opposite corner of the room.

Sara Ahmad

Ken Livingstone Has Collapsed

With the Burnham Plan of 1909 Chicago was built into a grid of diagonal streets and perpendicular arterials. The experience of walking through the city today is one of perpetual shock; intersections between two identical streets lined with tall buildings are sites of crises as the tourist realises that he has been silently locked into a network of logic. The working commute and the recreational pursuit are elegantly collapsed in the construction of the 'two-level' street. Driving a vehicle down Wacker Drive often evinces moments of confronting your fear of bats and dressing in a cape. The city of London, however, retains its square-mile medieval boundaries. Moving through the streets of the City one feels that the financial district has awkwardly imposed itself on *Londinium*. The Bank of England stands like a lost ship amidst the increasingly windy trails and buildings grow on pavements like unruly trees. Men in Armani walk into glass walls; women buy the Big Issue because it is Christmas and a hard time for everyone.

On the corner of East London Mosque Ken Livingstone collapsed. The pavement is the property of pigeons as it has over the years become covered in delicate bird sick and Socialist Workers Party tracts. All the headlines scream KEN LIVINGSTONE HAS COLLAPSED. Before he had stepped off the tube that morning he thought he saw the flash of a Cheshire smile in the glass pane of the window. At any point in London you are never more than ten feet away from a rat. George Galloway shook with feline laughter next to the London Wall while below where he stood twelve rodents made love to their sisters in the intricate network of Thames Water.

The London Wall is now merely a stretch of road trod by apathetic punters who enjoy reading the 'Weird' and 'Odd Balls' sections in the Metro. Just off one of the city's many 'piss alleys' there is a small cafe with an orange front and no other outstanding quality. Sat under a blurry painting of a bridge with water lilies is S.D., exuding all the discreet charm of the bourgeoisie from the bra which peaks out of her jumper. She is waiting for G.W. who is twenty minutes late. G.W. arrives at 12:54 after having missed the 12:46 at Liverpool Street and sits opposite her friend without ordering anything.

'Sorry I'm late.'

'You missed quite a lot. A great big bird flew in the door and shat everywhere because that's what they do when they're scared.'

'I was held up by a man who tried to get me signed up to the British Heart Foundation.'

'My grandfather died of a stroke! By the end of it he had to carry around a bag full of his urine.'

'Have you had lunch? I breakfasted on toothpaste

this morning and not much else.'

'God, are you eating properly? You look like an Irish nationalist. Have some of my muffin before you disappear. Where were you at dinner on Wednesday? E.V. drank an entire bottle and started talking about genocide.

'P.Q. was at dinner. I think B.D. invited her out of pity for her depressive episode. She was dressed like such a racist! Especially her hat. My dad was friends with her dad when we were younger and I invited her to my seventh birthday party. She just sat in the corner eating ham slices the whole time.

'She had a miscarriage last month and the father was the managing director of the company, I think.

'B.D. tried to mention it during dinner but I hushed him with a story about my dream where all my teeth fall out. He had burnt the mushroom risotto so tried to make us all do cocaine afterwards to make up for it. Do you reckon it's going to snow again today? I saw about three people fall down the steps at Waterloo station. The roads were ice.'

Before she had got off at Liverpool Street at 12:47 G.W. had looked through the window between Tottenham Court Road and Holborn to catch a glimpse of a ghost station as it hurtled by. Cast iron tunnels became bricks and then cast iron tunnels, as the disused British Museum Station illuminated like a memory by electric light and then faded with a hush as darkness descended once more upon the breathing sleeper trains. No passengers have alighted there since

1932. Closed stations and abandoned plans (Aldwych, St. Mary's) glint like portal keys to an imagined and real past, present, and future. Place is no longer a measure of distance but a dream labyrinth in which one could travel 300 miles by closing your eyes. Your mother is asking if you know where the remote is from the living room but you cannot reply because you are outside time and space. As she sat in the tube compartment G.W. imagined getting off at Aldwych in 1940 with someone she loved to see the Elgin Marbles while they were hidden in subterranean splendour from German bombardment.

'I wasn't at dinner because I went to see C.L.E. before he left for Luton.'

'Oh!'

'We arranged to meet outside the Tate but I was two hours late. He won't speak to me again.'

'What were you doing for two hours?'

'I caught the wrong train and ended up in some sort of infinite loop'

'He said he waited for forty minutes and then left'

'He had his back against the wall. It was cool and marble and the air nipped his face'

'I tried to tell him the last time I tried to speak of it but'

'It was minus four and my hands were ice'

'We watched a man dressed as a rat perform mime and then he said he had to go'

'He left on his bike and I walked to the station'

'I read a story about a shrine dedicated to the new

MP elect in Bradford Mosque in the paper on the way home'

'I got home and it was 22 degrees inside and I watched the ice caps melt on TV'

Contributors

SARA AHMAD has just finished studying English at Corpus Christi, Cambridge, and thinks her three years here were really quite nice. Her top three favourite men at the moment are Roland Barthes, Walter Benjamin and Michael Fassbender. She finds the experience of writing in the third person rather sad, like writing your own eulogy and sending out the invitations for the funeral because no one else wants to do it. Next year she will probably be unemployed.

SCOTT ANNETT has been at Cambridge for quite a while now. He's spent most of that time reading Dante and Levi and Beckett and Shakespeare in an energetic but not always very organized fashion. He's thinking about maybe finishing a PhD soon, and afterwards he would like to do fun things, like more teaching and talking and (if he's lucky) writing. This is the first time he's made it into the *Mays* and he's delighted because XX is a much rounder number than XVIII.

FELIX BAZALGETTE studies English at Fitzwilliam College, Cambridge. He's from London. He won four Tour de France stages, and wore the yellow jersey for six days in 1926.

LOUISE BENSON edited *Varsity* last term, launched her own magazine, *Hot and Cool,* two years ago – now distributed in the Tate Modern and Serpentine Gallery – and publishes her images and ideas at *louisebenson.blogspot.com*. She will be graduating this June.

ALICE BLACKHURST completed her undergraduate degree in Modern Languages at Emmanuel College, Cambridge in 2010. She then spent a year at Harvard studying fiction writing, American literature and art history. She is currently completing an MPhil in European Literature and will start a PhD in October.

ENRICO CIONI was born in Bologna, Italy, to an American mother and an Italian father. He spent his first year at Emmanuel College, Cambridge, studying Social and Biological Anthropology, as well as Archaeology. In his second year, he chose to specialise in Biological Anthropology, but, having decided that searching tropical undergrowth for howler monkey excrement is not all it's cracked up to be, he's now studying Archaeology. Enrico's first foray into writing was a fairly embarrassing novel entitled *There's A Lot That People Don't Know About Wolves*, which he wrote inspired by Chris Baty's book, *No Plot? No Problem!*

SUSIE CRONIN has a funny Irish accent according to the English, and a quare English accent according to the Irish. To the Malagasy and plenty others besides, she has the hair of a nocturnal sorceress, or less glamorously, someone in need of a good scrub; the luck of someone who shares a homeland with Westlife, and the portion control of someone slow to forget their agricultural background. She enjoys skating on ice but less so on cobblestones. She is reading Modern and Medieval Languages at King's College, Cambridge.

PHOEBE DICKERSON – a student of Pembroke College, Cambridge – first grasped a pencil at the age of two, to questionable literary effect. Brought up in London to the sounds of the metropolis, she now lives above a Co-op and in close proximity to cows. She is currently working towards a PhD on the subject of skin in 17th century verse.

MARIA DIMITROVA is a writer and postgraduate student at Cambridge, currently completing an MPhil in Screen Media and Cultures. She is an alumna of the Warwick Writing Programme and her writing has appeared in *The Telegraph*, *TANK*, *The Huffington Post UK*, *INK*, and *The Warwick Review*, among others. The published excerpt is from a longer project, which will hopefully turn into a complete novel at some point in the near future.

CHRYSTAL DING has just finished three years of English at Selwyn College. She took up photography five years ago as a way of rebelling against her Embarrassing Asian Tourist parents. Sadly this backfired and she now spends most of her time dodging punt tour guides. She is not – as people have assumed from her name – a stripper, porn star, six-foot-tall American blonde, or an advertisement for champagne flutes. But give it a few years.

LAWRENCE DUNN is a composer and improvising musician, who has just finished studying music at Corpus Christi College, Cambridge. He also takes photographs when he can.

ROWAN EVANS is from Bristol. His first chapbook, *returnsongs* (Wide Range, Cambridge), deals with lyric, earth material and sensory space. Rowan's work is influenced both by a British tradition that includes Basil Bunting, Barry MacSweeney and Maggie O'Sullivan, and by American poets such as e e cummings, George Oppen and Peter Gizzi. He studies English at Emmanuel College, Cambridge, where he also co-runs the poetry and drama event *Hatch*, and is current president of the English Society. His blog is *prospects for owl* (*rowanevans.blogspot.com*).

CHRISTINA FARLEY is a History of Art student at Cambridge, whose various interests include architecture, history, music, philosophy, rambling (in both senses of the word) and General Geekery. She plays the violin, but since it got out that she plays the viola too she's mainly been doing that instead. She likes liquorice, the colour green and libraries – libraries a bit too much.

ALEXANDER FREER has studied English literature at Warwick and Cambridge, and starts a PhD on Wordsworth's poetry and prose at Christ's College, Cambridge, this Autumn. His work most recently appeared in *Lung Jazz: Young British Poets for Oxfam*.

ADA GAFTER-O'HIGGINS was born and raised in New York City. She is a current undergraduate in Modern Languages at Wadham College, Oxford. She is interested in creative writing and theatre, having most recently collaborated with the New York based experimental theatre company Throes Theatre.

JIM KITCHEN has just finished his degree in English Literature. As a reward he is getting a long overdue haircut. He loves his family, friends and (among other things) ABBA, football and those toffee waffles you get in coffee shops. He plans to spend the rest of his summer watching *The Complete Collection of Alan Partridge* and listening to Fleetwood Mac. The future, as always, is unknown.

JESS KWONG recalls: Vancouver, coloring in a picture of the two ugly stepsisters while strangers moved into her house; Honolulu, the ex-con and the little orange; Princeton, filibustering, a cast party that ended in a group hug that ended six hours later; Michaum, figure eights in the tin monkey; Freetown, Ewart falling off the roof; Brooklyn, pound laundry, the day they found the body in McCarren Park Pool; Cambridge, the world map puzzle, the lampshade, and the waterglass.

EMMA LEVINKIND would like to write self-deprecating humour, but feels that she wouldn't be very good at it. She is a grammatical pedant, and hates it when people manage to somehow split infinitives, misplace aspos-trophe's, and end sentences with prepositions; it can't be put up with. She also dislikes pretentious self-referential jokes.

She is ostensibly studying geography at Hertford College, Oxford.

BETTY LIOU is an American (or rather, a New Yorker) who looks Chinese but wishes to be a cyborg who can occasionally unplug from consciousness. Besides being a professional daydreamer, graphic designer and wannabe artist, she has just finished her studies in Arts, Culture and Education from an unknown college called St Edmunds, nestled in the greater bubble known as Cambridge. When not squandering her school loans in a most unproductive way, she enjoys pondering over the wise mysterious words found in fortune cookies.

TOBY LLOYD's story 'Dave's Eleven' was published in *Mays XVIII*. Last year he was on the editorial team for *Mays XIX*. He is also the Vice President of the Oxford University Poetry Society. His story, 'Here, At the Still Point', was runner up in the *Oxonian Review* short story competition, and can be read on the *OR* website. He has just finished an English degree at Lady Margaret Hall.

CHLOE SPIBY LOH, coming from a family of artists, designers and architects, has always been interested in the arts. Before coming to Cambridge to do Architecture, she also completed a foundation course at Central Saint Martins in London. Particular interests lie within the photography, graphical arts and visual representation scene, typically from the beginning of the 20th century in Europe onwards.

ROBYN LOWE is reading English at Queens' College, Cambridge. Most of the literature she has studied so far has been pre-19th century but she has recently written a dissertation on the treatment of ritual and reflections in the works of Angela Carter. As well as writing poetry she is currently working on a collection of short stories and some short pieces of drama.

EMILY MARCHANT has just finished studying English at Newnham College, Cambridge. She has dabbled in writing since she was seven, at which tender age she was convinced that the literary world needed a fantasy novel about flying horses confronting a race of socio-pathic alien cyborgs. More recently, she's calmed down slightly.

IOANNA MAVROU writes short stories and novels and runs a tiny publishing house called Book Ex Machina. She just graduated from the Oxford Creative Writing course. She is currently working on her first novel, and a short story collection called *Stories from the End of the*

World. One day she'll learn how to play the ukulele, or to fly, or both.

JAMES MCKNIGHT is a poet with a grounding of deep roots in prose fiction. Try as he might, he has not been able to pull them up. Narrative lies under the skin of his poetry, and lyrical rhythms drive his prose. Beyond this, his preoccupations include desire and the unfulfilled, bodily dysphoria, dissatisfaction, birds and landscapes. He studies English Literature at Robinson College, Cambridge.

RICHARD O'BRIEN has written poetry and plays, including two musicals and one Edinburgh Fringe disaster. His first collection, *your own devices*, was published by tall-lighthouse press in 2009, and his work features in *The Salt Book of Younger Poets*. After finishing his degree in English and French at Brasenose College, Oxford, he will be working for a French radio station and translating the songs of Georges Brassens for a minimal crossover audience.

JAMIE PATTON is a third-year English student who has had pieces published in *Carillon*, *Varsity*, *The Dial*, *The Tower*, and *Veer*. He wrote and directed *Anderman* in Michaelmas of 2011, and his most recent play, *From the High Tower*, has been shortlisted for this year's Other Prize. He enjoys perversely mentioning – in biographies such as this one – that he has won two competitions for creating text-adventures, and that he wrote his third-year dissertation on interactive fiction, because 'they're fiction too!' Next year he will study Interactive Media at Goldsmith's, because he really is like a dog with a bone on this point.

CLEMMY PLEMING is studying English at St John's College, but much of that time is spent in the sweet embrace of video games, to the possible detriment of her studies. She also likes to draw and read comics. She hibernates every winter for three to six months and has a chitinous exoskeleton.

JACK SHACKLETON was born in Macclesfield and grew up in the Peak District. He really wants to be a superhero / fighter pilot / astronaut / albatross, but in the meantime he is studying German and Italian at Magdalen College, Oxford. His favourite writers are Ted Hughes, Raymond Carver, Rainer Maria Rilke, and Italo Calvino.

CLAUDIA STOCKER is a masters student in systems biology and the founder of the Cambridge student design society camGraphik. She has been an illustrator and graphic designer for most of her four years at Cambridge, and plans to make a career of it after graduation. She is hoping to eventually specialise in a field that allows her to combine both her creative and analytical sides, such as data visualisation or science communications. Her entry for the *Mays* is part of a series drawn at the Royal College of Surgeons'

Hunterian museum. More information may be found at *www.claudiastocker.com*.

JONAS L. TINIUS, born 1989, studies Social Anthropology at the University of Cambridge. He works on the intersections between anthropology, philosophy, and theatre near his hometown in the Ruhr area of Germany. He publishes with the London-based Hill Magazine, and has translated poetry and written for the American journal of translation *Aldus*, and the German *Brink* magazine. Selected visual workings can be explored on *assemblingaffects.blogspot.com*.

GEORGIA R. WAGSTAFF spends some of her time reading English at Girton College, Cambridge, but mostly can be found trying to act and trying to write. Her influences include D.G. Rossetti, Edward Lear, Baudelaire, Plath, Hughes, musician Patrick Wolf and 'environmental poets' such as Alice Oswald and Peter Larkin. Georgia would tell you her favourite time to write is under the moon at midnight, but it's too cliché and so shan't be allowed. Georgia recently had a small chapbook published, titled *Sycamore*, and more of her work can be found at *georgiaraphael.blogspot.co.uk*. This poem is not about butterflies.

The intrepid TIM WATERS, fresh from studying English at Emmanuel College Cambridge, is now bound for London to seek his fortune as a lawyer. He enjoys music, travelling, languages, history, and the fine particularity of how light falls on things. His literary influences include Geoffrey Hill, Italo Calvino, and Michael Longley. He hopes to keep writing, and to write better.

Next year EMMA WOODWARD will be completing her final year of Part I Architecture. Her current studies are an extension of interests manifested during her previous four years of fine art education. Spatial practices and the materiality of the physical are interests that have driven her sculptural practice; now such interests are crossing over into her architectural thinking and design work.

LEWIS WYNN is a first year English student at Emmanuel College, Cambridge. Born and raised in South London, the city and its temperament supersaturate his work, composed with ink and patience on thick granular paper. He hopes this piece will slowly expand and extend into a fuller work. He has recently suffered from an unfortunate haircut, and enjoys cinema, an industry he aspires to work in.

ALICE ZOO is self-taught photographer from Suffolk, currently studying French and Spanish at St. Hugh's College, Oxford. She started taking pictures to indulge her nostalgia, and now uses photography as a medium through which to impress her way of seeing on others. Influences include Francesca Woodman, Paolo Roversi and Emma Hardy. She is planning to spend her year abroad, studying photography in Paris. Alice hopes that one day her pictures will encourage other people to want to take pictures too.